JESUS TOUCHED ME AND MADE ME WHOLE

A TRUE LIFETIME STORY AND TESTIMONY

CHRISTINE MBONENYE OSAHON

ACKNOWLEGEMENT

Now I bow down at the feet of The Lord Jesus Christ to thank God The Father and God The Son and God The Holy Spirit; for having healed me, saved me and made me witness to God's Saving power and healing power; by writing this book to proclaim the Good News of The Kingdom of God. I hereby announce to you people of God that the Kingdom of God is here! To God be the glory, honour, power, wisdom, blessings forever and ever. I am a living testimony for the glory of God by His Son Jesus Christ who touched me and made me whole – body, spirit and soul. I love God with all my heart, my soul and my strength. I love Jesus because He first loved me.

It is by the grace of God that we are saved and I believe I am a product and a living testimony of what the grace of God can do in our midst.

I am forever grateful for God's grace because Jesus Christ is forever faithful to me.

INTRODUCTION

Every one of my readers might have an issue that might clinch them deep down their lives; let it be hurts, emotions, sickness, financial, politics, ministry and business, worries and troubles of life whether it is for self or beloved ones. The ultimate answer is there is nothing impossible for God, what is impossible for men; with God it is possible. (Matthew 19:26; Jeremiah 32:17, 26-27; Luke 1:37)

As a child of God, nothing should barricade you or stop you from accomplishing your dreams in life. Do not allow the customs and laws of your origins or environment to limit you. Don't be constrained by the conventional thoughts and beliefs or norms of your community, neither by failures of those who were before you.

Be positive right from the core of your mind and recognise that God can do a new thing through you! There are so many things that people of old never contemplated about to happen, but God did them before their own eyes and we still read and believe in those miracles that were performed of long ago by the power of God. For example, No ninety year old woman has ever been impregnated by a ninety-nine year old man, but it happened to Abraham and his wife. Secondly, no one had ever split a sea or river, but Moses and Joshua in the Bible, they did. Thirdly, no one had ever conceived by the power of the Holy Spirit, but Virgin Mother Mary conceived Jesus by the power of the Holy Spirit. And most of all no man had ever seen the dead raised except the ones Jesus raised from the dead. And Jesus Christ died but on the third day He rose again from the dead by the power of God.

Remember that God is willing to help you today, and He is ready to do new and glorious things in your life if you avail yourself and open your heart to receive him today. Understand that you can lay hold of whatever miracle you desire in your life today; for it is written: "For truly I say to you, that whoever shall say to this mountain, be you removed and be cast into the sea; and shall not doubt in his heart, but shall believe that those things which he said shall come to pass; he shall have whatever he said." (Mark 11:23)

TRIBUTE

Honouring parent is a godly thing, so I would like to pay tribute to my beloved parents for their love, moral support, guidance and tender care and being there in the times I needed you most!! You stood with me through thick and thin. More abundant life and I love you beyond measure.

All of my sweetest parents and dear siblings I love you always, thank you for crying with me, laughing with me, joking with me, understanding me, your overprotective attitudes were a sign of love and care, looking after me and you my elder siblings thanks for guiding me. All my family thanks for shared joy and moments of being a family; the struggle of pain during my sickness by praying for me, loving me, and caring for me. God bless you all and those who are still alive I pray for more divine protection, long life and abundant blessings of God upon our lives and families. Those who passed to eternity may their souls rest in eternal peace.

I would like to thank all the servants of God who prayed for me and ministered to me even before I received Christ; this was a seed you sowed and somebody else watered and now it has germinated and had fruits in the Kingdom of God. Siblings and friends/college mates of my youth who allowed me to preach to them and lead them to Jesus Christ in my early days of Salvation; let us continue to cling on to the rugged Cross and trust the Lord and our Saviour Jesus Christ; the Messiah.

I would like to pay tribute to the men and women of God who ministered to me as a young believer while in East Africa mostly in Uganda, especially at Watoto Church Central (aka Kampala Pentecostal Church) which was my first Church, as a born again young person of the 1990s.

I do not forget the men and women of God in the UK especially Alpha and Omega, Christ Faith Tabernacle Church, Agape Miracle Centre and Liberty Christian Fellowship Church, who have ministered to me as I grew in the Lord; and also allow me to serve humbly, this is just a beginning; we are still serving in the vineyard of our Lord Jesus Christ until he comes back. I also thank God for my Pastor Lincoln A.K Serwanga (Apostle) of Liberty Christian Fellowship London for praying for me, mentoring me for the past ten years; and helping me to structure this book.

I also thank God for my best half and best friend - my husband for companionship. Thanks for your love and support. I pray for more abundant life for both of us in the Kingdom of God. May our Lord Jesus Christ continue to bless us to serve God together by his grace all the days of our lives and until he comes back. Goodness and mercy always to follow us. I love you!

All Scripture quotations are taken from the King James
Version of the Bible. (Both paperback and online via
media apps)

ISBN 978-0-9955082-0-0

Published by Christine Mbonenye Osahon Publishing

Website: http://moralsc21.simplesite.com

Cover design by Catford Printers

PRINTED IN THE UNITED KINGDOM – LONDON

FORWARD

Once in a life time we all have a story to tell, we have also heard about the story of the woman with the issue of blood in the Bible, the story of John the Baptist, and of course the story of our Lord Jesus Christ; how he came to die for me and you for our sins. My wife Christine, have been busy for so many years now trying to tell her story on a one to one basis, about how she was touched by our Lord Jesus and she became whole again, after some kind of illness that was about to disturb her as teenager. She has come up with her story written in this book, to let all the believers out there who are looking for miracles to be rest assured, that the God of yesterday is still the God of today, and God forevermore will he be. He can do all things beyond our imagination.

This is a book of testimonies and inspirations, what you will read in this book will inspire you to know that our Lord liveth. Read this book and be immersed in the Word of God and every obstacle will give way to freedom.

She has witnessed miracles, as God redeemed something from ashes to gold. Every step of the way has been accompanied by her prayers and this book has been written from her experience over the years. I can say I am very privileged to have such a great woman of God besides me.

Your all and only sincere husband,

Daniel.

DEDICATION

This book is dedicated with love to my only Lord and personal Saviour Jesus Christ, the lover of my soul, who saved me, touched me and healed me and made me whole again, by giving me a new and abundant life in the Kingdom of God. You are the reason I live, to testify the goodness of the Lord in the land of the living.

I love you Jesus, because you are the one who first loved me with an everlasting love. You are a miracle worker Jesus Christ the Son of the Living God and saviour of the world.

CONTENTS

CHAPTER ONE

THE HEALING AND SAVING POWER OF JESUS CHRIST

There are great healings and breakthrough power in the mighty name of Jesus Son of the Holy and true one of Israel – The Almighty God. The Holy Spirit is the power of God there to help us, sanctify us and fulfil the word of God in us. The Word of God never changes and abides forever. Jesus Christ is the same yesterday, today and forevermore. As he used to work in the times of his walking planet earth and working through his prophets and apostles and servants, He still work even now through his everlasting word – which is true and faithful. There is healing in that name of Jesus; there is deliverance in that name, there is breakthrough still in that name above all names. If anyone is seeking to be touched, there is first-hand evidence in The Holy word of God the Bible. And my favourite verse, which is "Mark 5:25-34 the woman was healed of the issue of blood.

"Now a certain woman had a flow of blood for twelve years, and had suffered many things from many physicians. She had spent all that

she had and was no better, but rather grew worse. When she heard about Jesus, she came behind him in the crowd and touched the tassel of his garment. For she said, "If only I may touch the tassel of his clothes, I shall be made well." Immediately the fountain of her blood was dried up, and she felt in her body that she was healed of the affliction. And Jesus, immediately knowing in himself that power / virtue had gone out of him, turned around in the crowd and said, "Who touched my clothes?" But his disciples said to him, "You see the multitude thronging you and you say, 'who touched me?'" And Jesus looked around to see her who had done this thing. But the woman, fearing and trembling, knowing what had happened to her came and fell down before him and told him the whole truth. And Jesus said to her, "Daughter, your faith has made you whole / well. Go in peace, and be healed of your affliction." (Mark 5:25-34; NKJV)

It is only Jesus Christ who can free us from all our sufferings and afflictions as we have read the above holy Scriptures. For the first time in the Word of God, where it is written that a person; moreover a woman touched Jesus, and his power healed her; whereas in most cases we see that it is Jesus Christ who touches or lays hands on people, and they get healed. This woman's faith made the miraculous move in an extraordinary way, because; Jesus permitted it that way. There is nothing too difficult for God; He is the Lord of all flesh as his Word tells us in the Bible in the book of Jeremiah 32 verse 26.

Faith in God heals; this is the mind-set you have got to have

Having worked up herself by using human effort to get healed, "the woman with the issue of blood" as she is referred to in the Bible, no name was given to her because this is an extraordinary miracle. She touched Jesus while it was Jesus who usually touches us but it is all the same hand of the Holy Spirit who touches us in our mind, thoughts, spirit or heart to reach out to meet with Jesus by aligning our thoughts to the godly feelings of faith in God. The woman with the issue of blood made up her mind, and she became determined, she made a decision and focused with a mind-set to prepare her heart to receive an instant miracle by Faith from The LORD Jesus. The woman was not scared of what other people would think of her. She wholly put all her belief and trust in getting healed on that day without any distractions or barriers from humans and other traditional obstacles of not going to the public places while with that ill-health as it was forbidden by her Jewish customs and culture!

She was determined to receive her miracle against all odds, and the Lord, who knows the intents and motives of men, had already seen her secret intentions, of her desperation and faith in Jesus to get healed. Therefore Jesus created a way and permitted her to touch him and instantly the issue of blood was dried up and healed, right there! Oh, what a mighty God we trust and serve and obey! He is merciful and kind and even longsuffering that when we suffer, Jesus suffers with us, and he is always willing to help and heal us if we allow him.

Jesus saves and heals lives.

Now dear brother or sister, what is bothering you? Is it sickness or some other life's troubles? Give your life to God by receiving Jesus Christ as your LORD and Saviour and the LORD can give you a new life right there where you are at now. The Word of God says in John 3:16 that, *"For God so loved the world, that he gave us his only begotten beloved Son, Jesus Christ, that whosoever believes in him will never perish but have eternal life."*

Therefore, people of God, it is imperative to believe and set your mind to do as the Holy Bible says. In Romans 10:8-12: *"The word is near you, in your mouth and in your heart, that is: the word of faith which we preach; that if*

*you confess with your mouth the LORD Jesus
and believe in your heart that God has raised
him from the dead, you will be saved."*

Salvation

Salvation is the life of God in man's spirit. You
can pray, believe and put your faith entirely in
God's hands. His arms are widely open to
embrace you and receive you now through
Jesus Christ his Son; who is the way, the
truth and life (John 4:6).

"Sozo" is the original Greek word (verb) in the
new testament meaning to save (*saved*), heal,
cure, to make whole, rescue from danger, to
cause something to change to an earlier or
correct or appropriate state, to renew, to
restore, or to redeem. That is what Jesus
Christ did for you and me at the cross of
Calvary, because of the fall of Adam and Eve
in Genesis 3 (*you can read it*). All humans and
the whole world were under a curse, and man
was separated from our original glory from
God. Adam and Eve were cast out of the
Garden of Eden (Paradise on Earth) to suffer
consequences of afflictions, pain, death,
sicknesses, crime, hate, wars, famine, hard
work and labour, etc. (*Read Genesis 3).* God
sent us his only begotten Son Jesus Christ the
Messiah who came to **SAVE** or **Sozo** (*see the
Greek meaning*) us all by dying on the cross,

and resurrecting after three days (*John 3:16-17*) and went to heaven interceding for us always (paraphrasing Romans 8:31-34)

"Sozo" has a (noun) in Greek and its noun is **"Soteria"** translated in the New Testament as the English word **Salvation.** Ephesians 2:8: *"By grace are you saved through faith, not by our works no one can boost."*

Is there any situation that had been difficult to surrender? And it has been resisting your prayers? Try to go deeper in your faith; launch your nets in the deep and you will catch more fish. We see Simon Peter believed in Jesus when he had toiled all night and had caught nothing. But at his Word do it and get closer into an intimate relationship by allowing Jesus into your life (boat) and sail this world together through storms, dry seasons, and darkness Jesus will calm your sea (life) with peace and make your life meaningful by catching fish (prosperity, salvation). He will light your dark world with shining. You need to be restored and make your relationship with Christ even deeper; let him be the centre of your focus, the rest will be history, and you will testify like Simon Peter. *(Luke 5:4-11).*

Do not have any doubt but have faith in God and just tell that mountain to move from here to cast itself in the sea and it shall be so *(Mark*

11:23). Jesus is calling your name today, and he is eagerly waiting to receive you. There is no tomorrow to get saved, the time for salvation is now, tomorrow will never come. Let him enter into your heart, your life, your household and business today, that stubborn sickness will go; that debt will be solved and the court case or any matters that bother and trouble you will be okay- if you allow him into your life.

He (Jesus) is right now standing and knocking at your door, do not harden your heart, soften your heart and let him enter in and touch you today and save you. He says, *"Behold; I stand at the door and knock. If anyone hears my voice and opens the door, I will come in to him and dine with him and him with me"*. *(Revelation 3:20)*

Please let us lay some foundation about how heaven operates and some things related to judgement and what will happen during the end of life.

Heaven and Hell are both real

God will judge the secrets and actions of men by the ruling of Jesus Christ. Friends, you need to put right your life, and if you are walking uprightly in Christ Jesus, make sure you abide in him. Everyone will be judged according to his works; whether secretly or openly, all are registered by God. It is worth to know this and live your life correctly and appropriately. The Word of God says only those saved, who have their names written in the Lamb's Book of Life, will live and when they die they will go to heaven. However, unrepentant people will go to hell when they die. *(Revelation 21:22-27)*

The great white throne of Judgement

Unbelievers are punished by God for their unbelief; so someone needs to know now if you were ignorant of this. You might think that it is an old fashion way of preaching heaven and hell, but don't be deceived, both are real, and God rewards every man according to their decisions and actions. Now the word is on your tongue and your heart, believe in Jesus Christ and live, or unbelievers has consequences of going to hell when they die. And remember that no one knows the time and calendar of their life; it is all in the hands of the Creator God. Jesus is also coming back anytime, and no one knows the time or the hour or the year; therefore, I encourage you today not to harden your heart and if you are in Christ Jesus, continue. This is expressed more in the scriptures as follows:

"And the devil that deceived them was cast into the lake of fire and brimstone, where the

beast and the false prophet are, and shall be tormented day and night for ever and ever. Then I saw a great white throne and him who sat on it, from whose face the earth and the heaven fled away. And there was found no place for them. And I saw the dead, small and great, standing before God, and books were opened. And another book was opened, which is the book of Life. And the dead were judged according to their works, by the things which were written in the books. The sea gave up the dead who were in it, and death and hades delivered up the dead who were in them. And they were judged, each one according to his works. Then death and hades were cast into the lake of fire. This is the second death. And anyone not found written in the book of life was cast into the lake of fire." (Revelation 20:10-15)

Today, you have an opportunity to receive Jesus Christ; you receive life and eternal life. The bible emphasises about getting saved and receiving Jesus Christ here it is written: *"But what saith it? The word is near thee, even in your mouth, and in your heart: that is the word of faith, which we preach; that if you shall confess with your mouth the Lord Jesus, and shall believe in your heart that God has raised him from the dead, you shall be saved. For with the heart man believes unto righteousness; and with the mouth confession is made unto salvation. For the scripture says, whosoever believes on him shall not be ashamed." Romans 10:8-11.* You shall be saved.

Confess this prayer after me:

"Dear Lord Jesus, I believe you are the Son of God; and you died for me, to take away and forgive my sins, please dear Lord, forgive me all my sins and wash away all my transgressions, cleanse me and purify me. Erase my name from the book of death and write my name in the book of life. I now invite you to be Lord over my life, and I am born-again. Fill me with your Spirit. Thank You, Jesus, for saving me - In the mighty name of the Father, the Son and the Holy Spirit. Amen."

Born-again John 3:16

Now you are a born-again Christian that is what Jesus talked about when he said in John 3:3 to Nicodemus, *"Most assuredly, I say to you unless one is born again, he cannot see or enter into the Kingdom of God."* Now you have become a born-again by inviting Christ into your life, as you believed in your heart and confessed with your lips that God raised him from the dead. And that Jesus Christ is the begotten Son of God and a Saviour of the world. You confessed and have received salvation, it is free, and it is the life of God.

You are now a candidate of the Kingdom of God. It is written: *"But as many as received him, to them gave he the power to become the sons of God; even to them that believe on his name. Which were born, not of blood, nor of the will of the flesh, nor of the will of man, but of God?"* *(John 1:12-13)* now you have been transformed, and he sends his Holy Spirit to live within you, and a transformation starts from inside out. *(1John 4:4)*

When you become a Christian, you start to love other Christians, and you need to bond with other Christians and fellowship with them. *1John 5:4* says that when you become a Christian, you cross the line you are now born of God and out of the world (overcame the world), a Christian is known by the way you live your life. And when one is born of God he does not sin and no evil can touch him *(1John 5:18)* now you have, and you live an eternal life. Jesus says, *"Behold, I stand at the door and knock. If anyone hears my voice and opens the door, I will come in to him and dine with him, and he with me. To him who overcomes I will grant to sit with me on my throne, as I also overcame and sat down with my father on his throne."* *(Revelation 3:20-21)*

Having become a born-again Christian, do make a step of faith and be bold to announce your faith in Jesus Christ publicly by telling one or two people about the decision you have just made. The Lord made me understand it from an early age of my salvation, and I knew straight away that it comes with a blessing attached to it. It is a spiritual act and a good thing because Jesus Christ speaks about it as he said: *"Whosoever, therefore, shall confess me before men, him will I confess also before my father who is in Heaven. But whosoever shall deny me before men, him will I also deny before my father which is in heaven."* Matthew *10:32-33.* Also, our Lord Jesus encourages us that when he speaks to us and saves us in secret (darkness); that we should speak it in the light: and what you hear in the ear, that preach you on the housetops."*(Matthew 10:27).* That is why I will not keep silent until Jerusalem is established a praise in the earth; (Isaiah 62:6-7). It is the Lord that commands us we are his watch men and women in the Kingdom of heaven here on planet earth.

Furthermore, this is an act of Evangelising to your peers, or friends, family and relatives or workmates. The Bible says in *Romans* 10:14-15; *"How then shall they call on Him in whom they have not believed? And how shall they believe in Him of whom they have not heard? And how shall they hear without a preacher? And how shall they preach unless they are sent? As it is written: "How beautiful are the feet of those who preach the gospel of peace, which bring glad tidings of good things!"*

You keep calling on the name of Jesus, praying to God the Father through him and reading the Holy Word of God from the Bible and as well as listening to the hymns and inspirational Christian songs. If you lived your life in an unworthy Christian style, that is in sin. You need to forsake your old ways of life because now you are a new creation in Christ Jesus as it is written in *2Corinthian 5:17; "Therefore, if anyone is in Christ Jesus, he is a new creation; old things have passed away; behold, all things have become new. Now I am an ambassador of Jesus Christ."*

Please, you make sure to keep calling on the name of Jesus and pleading his precious blood upon your life. Surely know that you are a child of God, and your past is no more according to the Word of God we have just seen above; you are now a new creation in Christ Jesus.

If you are hurting or have any sickness in your body you have to read our opening verse; *Mark 5:25-34.* Continue prayer with other Word of God relating to your problem, and also take a step of faith to believe in your spirit or heart that Jesus Christ has touched you because of the finished work on the cross and start to thank him for healing you. The finished work Jesus did on the cross at Calvary is written in Isaiah 53:4-5;

"Surely He (Jesus Christ) has borne our griefs and carried our sorrows; yet we esteemed him stricken, smitten by God, and afflicted. But he was wounded for our transgression, he was bruised for our iniquities; the chastisement for our peace was upon him, and by his (Jesus) stripes we are healed."

The work has already been done for us and finished on the cross at Calvary over 2000 years ago. Now you need to tap into this finished work of grace by believing in Jesus Christ who is the author and the finisher of our faith. *(See Hebrews 12:2)*

God holds your life today and forever more! The "Most Powerful" and "Holy One" in the universe cares for you and your beloved ones and watches over you all constantly *(see Psalm 121:3: "I will lift up my eyes unto hills, from whence cometh my help. My help comes from the LORD, which made heaven and earth. He will not suffer thy foot to be moved: He that keeps thee will not slumber.")*. Don't live life worrying about your past, present or your future – live life knowing that God is in you, with you, and for you, every moment of the day no matter the circumstances!

You have been equipped by the Creator of the universe to overcome every obstacle. Forget what you lack. Look up to God, who loves you in Jesus Christ. The same power (*The Holy Spirit);* that raised Christ from the dead lives inside of you *(see Romans 8:11).* You are well able; you are anointed to accomplish your dreams just stay in the Lord.

Faith – how do I know?

One might have a question; "How do I know that I am healed?" The answer is that I hope you remember in our study Scripture in *Mark 5:25-34.* The woman with the issue of blood had made up her mind and decided to follow Jesus that alone was enough. She had to receive her healing that instant, if she could only touch the tassel or the thread of the garment of Jesus our Lord! She had already heard other people's testimonies as you are now reading mine in this book! Come on now!

She defied the Jewish culture by coming out of her house when she was unclean, and some other current customs do not allow women to mix up with men. But Jesus is a male, and the woman had to press through the entire male crowd; and twelve Apostles who surrounded Jesus. She put aside the consequences of breaking and tampering with culture and protocol; she needed a miracle of healing, and it was in Jesus as she had faith and believed that if only she could touch a small thread of His garment, she would be healed. The Word of God says that what you think in your heart is what you are *(Proverbs 23:7)*; or what you confess and believe is what is done unto you or what you become; "Out of the abundance of the heart the mouth speaks". *(Paraphrasing Luke 6:45)*

Now this is called **faith;** as it is written in *Hebrews 11:1; "Now faith is the substance of things hoped for, the evidence of things not seen. For by it the elders obtained a good testimony."* If you want to go into detail about what is faith, you can read all the Chapter of *Hebrews 11. "Without faith it is impossible to please God". (Hebrews 11:6).* I believe that the woman with the issue of blood had got faith, and she pleased God by believing in Jesus as her only source of healing, even though she had struggled with doctors and other physicians! The lady might have been poor and bankrupt because the disease had afflicted her for 12 years! Even relatives might have been fed up with her, the husband had already left her, and even neighbours couldn't come into her close contact because she was termed as unclean according to the Jewish tradition. *But thanks be to God for the victories that he gives us through Jesus Christ our Lord. (Corinthians 15:57).* I have been there until when Jesus had to meet with me, and now I am Queen Esther of my generation! God is respecter of no persons (Romans 2:9-11); he loves us. We are His children when we receive Jesus Christ as our Lord and Saviour and get salvation. *(See John 1:12; Romans 8:14-15)*

Specify your need by faith

By practising faith, a believer has to make up his or her mind to hope for the best results to yield or to see a picture of what you want to happen as a finished product; it is a mind-set. In other words, have a clear picture of yourself being touched by Jesus and see yourself healed as the woman with the issue of blood perceived. This is termed as *"to specify your need"*. The woman with the issue of blood specified her need. By focusing that if only she touches the thread of the Master Jesus' garment. However, Hannah at Shiloh decided to speak in tongues in the Church (Temple) and Prophet Eli perceived she was drunk. But Hannah prayed and vowed to God, *"If you give me a male child I will give him back to you to serve you, and no razor will touch his head"* *(paraphrasing 1Samuel 1:10-20)*. If you are praying for pregnancy to have a child, see yourself pregnant and then start to see your baby at birth all through into his or her life. If it's a ministry you believe God for; see yourself preaching to crowds and reaching out to many in Evangelism or healing.

You have to think faithful and be trustful that God has done it even after the prayers; be expectant. Do an act of faith and check yourself where it is hurting and have a gratitude heart full of thanks. For example, *Mark 5:28, "The woman thought; "If I only touch his garment I shall be healed".* Please note that in her thought there was no negativity, the woman created a space of positivity or faith. She was optimistic and she had a positive attitude towards Jesus and his divine Power. I hope this lady had a revelation that; *"Christ is the Visible image of the Invisible God, and that all things were created for him and by him they exist; and in Jesus everything in heaven and on earth has its proper place;"* so is my Prophetess Hannah in believing for a male child in 1Samuel chapter 1. (Colossians 1:17)

The woman with the issue of blood had no negative emotions or negative attitude neither for herself nor Jesus. She had faith and had a two-way dimension. These days you will hear some people saying in discouragement; "I know God is there, but the miracles don't happen." Such is a negative attitude because one is already faithless and he or she doesn't trust in God to do mighty miracles and wonders. That is what hinders their breakthrough, such as; healing that person's body or help them in any troublesome circumstances one might be facing. When we examine the Scriptures, we find out that "The Father of Faith" is Abraham.

God accounted it to him (Abraham) for righteousness, for believing on him that even at 100 years God can still make him healthy. *Genesis 15:6; "After these things the word of the LORD came unto Abraham in vision saying, Fear not Abram: I am thy shield, and thy exceeding great reward. And Abram said, Lord GOD, what will thou give me, seeing I go childless, and the steward of my house is this Eliezer of Damscus? And Abram said, Behold t me thou hast given no seed: and lo, one born in my house is mine heir. And behold, the word of the LORD came unto him, saying, This shall not be thine heir; but he that shall come forth out of thine own bowels shall be thine heir. And he brought him forth abroad, and said, Look now toward heaven, and tell the stars, if thou be able to number them: and he said unto him, So shall thy seed be. And he believed in the LORD; and he counted it to him for righteousness."* And his wives Sarah at 90 years to give her fertility and rejuvenate her hormones like a young woman; to give them Isaac, a son of the promise. This came to pass as it is written in the Bible: *"And the LORD visited Sarah as he had said, and the LORD did unto Sarah as he had spoken. For Sarah conceived, and bare Abraham a son in his old age, at the set time of which God had spoken to him. And Abraham called the name of his son that was born unto him, whom Sarah bare him, Isaac. And Abraham circumcised his son Isaac being eight days old, as God had commanded him. And Abraham was an hundred years old, when his son Isaac was born unto him. And Sarah said, God hath made me to laugh, so that all that hear will laugh with me." (Genesis 21:1-6)* Our God is awesome indeed! He turns nothing into something precious to display his glory! That is what God did; *"He turned the cross which the heathen that are perishing call foolishness and made it life, power and wisdom of God for us who are saved"! (1Corinthians 1: 18-25)*

We must know that we need to live by faith and walk by faith not by sight. Abraham walked by faith in God and this pleased God. Truly, God is very unpleased with a person who has no faith, so it is written that Faith pleases God, however; *"Without faith, it is impossible to please God; because anyone who comes to him must believe that he exists and that he rewards those who diligently seek him." (Hebrew 11:6)* As our book focuses on the opening verses of *Mark 5:25-34;* in this scripture, we critically discover that God rewarded the woman who had a blood issue because of his love for someone who has faith. Faith involves grace of God, which is the undeserved favour from God not of our works and no one could even boast about it! It is written in *Ephesians 2:8-9: "For by grace you have been saved through faith, and that not of yourselves; it is the gift of God, not of works lets anyone should boast."*

Our Lord Jesus was pleased with this lady; she knew that grace had come to her, yet she is a sinner and did not deserve it, but God had mercy on her. Nevertheless, this woman earnestly desired to seek the face of God through Jesus Christ. And she was rewarded with a gift of complete healing making her body whole again and a brand new life of being saved (born-again) was pronounced on her life and deposited in her spirit the moment Jesus declared; *"Daughter, your faith has made you whole or well. Go in peace and be healed of your affliction."* The woman was already healed, but she received salvation by grace through faith at the declaration of our Lord and master of her healing in the Bible in the book of Mark 5:34.

A believer should not be distracted by the storm or negativity of the hard circumstances he or she is going through. This is the trick of the devil to distract you in order to take your focus, and when you lose focus from trusting or worshipping God, you stray and give your attention to the liar, the devil and that means you doubt and that is worshipping the devil, thinking that The Lord cannot help you or has taken too long. Nothing deserves your worship but YAHWEH, no matter what the situation maybe. Therefore, do not be distracted, have faith in God and also have faith in Jesus as he taught us in his Word in the Bible in the Book of John 14:1 it is written: *"Let not your heart be troubled: ye believe in God, believe also in me."*

CHAPTER TWO

AVOID DISTRACTIONS FOCUS ON GOD

Avoid distractions, focus on Jesus

We have what is called the "Race of Faith" as it is written *"Therefore we also, since we are surrounded by so great a cloud of witnesses, let us lay aside every weight, and the sin which so easily ensnares us, and let us run with endurance the race that is set before us. Looking unto Jesus, the author and the finisher of our Faith, who for the joy that was set before him endured the cross, despising the shame, and has sat down at the right hand of the throne of God (Hebrews 12:1-2)."*

Some holy things are worth to go through shame and pain to get the crown of victory. For such as Jesus was betrayed by someone he trusted and loved like Judas Iscariot. He was bounded, and handed over to sinners and gentiles like Romans and their Judge Pontius Pilate, by his own Jews and chief priests. He was spat at, mocked, stripped 39 lashes of thorns at the weeping post, beaten; he was disfigured, despised and disowned by his Jewish leaders; so he was murdered by a painful and shameful death by crucifixion at the cross. Through it all, Jesus did not complain, yet he felt the pain and emotions as he was fully man. All of this, he endured for you and me and the entire world that we may receive Salvation. *(Isaiah 53:1-5; Mathew 27)*.

Ooh yeah! He is our model, to show us and encourage us that *"we can do all things through Jesus Christ who strengthens us."* *(Philippians 4:13)*.

For these reason brethren, when you have a good thought of following Jesus and seeking him with all your heart; you don't allow any distractions. What you do is to fix all your undivided attention to Jesus, (Heb 12:2); in the same manner this woman who had a blood issue did. She must have been mocked and not allowed to come into public. And also ashamed of this kind of disease, but she was encouraged to step forward and seek the Lord! She refused any barriers to barricade her or stop her from meeting our Lord; as she had heard all the miracles and good deeds that Jesus was doing everywhere, he went. She heard that he turned water into wine at a wedding in Cana *(John 2)*; resurrected the dead and healed the sick, the lame walked, the blind eyes opened, the deaf hear again, and the dumb spoke and chased demons away from people. *(Acts 10:38; Matthew 4, John 5:5-14)*

We should know that wherever the Lord Jesus is called and welcomed, he performs miracles, transforms and changes lives for life and eternity. I believe this, tasted it, living it and I sincerely encourage you to consider it from me. That is why this woman knew that wherever Jesus, "The Greatest Man" that ever walked on the planet Earth, was surrounded by the protocol of his disciples as the religious Pharisees of the time were seeking after to malice him. She walked by faith and refused to be distracted by neither the Pharisees nor the protocol but focused on Jesus, in doing so she was seeking the face of God to heal her. She knew that Jesus welcomed sinners, the sick, out-casts, the mis-understood, the poor, the destitute, the barren, the lame, the blind, the deaf, the demon-possessed and the gentiles. Furthermore, Jesus Christ did not discriminate anyone whom they termed as unclean because he cleansed them. Even leapers were cleansed by him and are still being cleansed today. Even now I know very well that every man has their leprosy that suffering or an issue that they would not want anyone to know like the prominent Syrian Army Officer Naaman. *(See 2Kings 5)*

However, I would like to inform you truly that he who sees in secret knows all your problems just take it to the Lord in prayer; it is well with your soul. Jesus will not leave you nor forsake you. As he is standing wide his arms open calling to you: *"Come all of you who are heavy laden and labour and I will give you rest." (Mathew 11:28)*. The woman with the issue of blood got rest from Jesus Christ and so do I.

You know that there is protocol in your Church not to shout, or move forward, or dance to the tune of the Lord, or to play your tambourine in worship, because some people are still maintaining their so-called diplomatic looks or stature. Or the Pastor might have bouncers who will bounce you back not to go closer to the altar when there are preaching or singing; just don't mind about that protocol, lift up your heart and lift up your eyes to the Lord and his heavens from whence your help come from and focus on Jesus. *(Paraphrasing, Psalm121)*. This is a heart to heart with the Lord, and you can only touch the heart of God and please him by faith. This is what is termed as "Worshipping God in spirit and in truth, and now is the time that our Lord and the Lord's Messiah prophesied in John 4:23-24, as it is written: *"But the hour cometh, and now is, when the true worshippers shall worship the Father in spirit and in truth: for the Father seeketh such to worship him God is a Spirit: and they that worship him must worship him in spirit and in truth.* Leave religion and build a personal relationship with God through Jesus Christ his Son by receiving salvation, and also get deeper in faith.

The same woman who is our study scripture refused to be distracted by protocol; she knew Jesus is merciful and will plead for her and remove all obstacles; so she was not afraid to break the barriers as she was convicted this was her time now to come out of darkness and obscurity into the marvellous light. *(Paraphrasing, 1Peter 2: 9).*

Touch Jesus by your faith as he touched you by his Grace: (*Mark 5: 29-30*)

It means that whenever you feel a desire or urge and nag to go to Christ or make any step of faith, you should act quickly. And know that the Lord has chosen you to be touched by his power or healing and divine transformation. Therefore; just break loose and beat all odds that are opposing your stepping forward; to make a step of faith to get up to pray or go to Church or read a scripture or fast or sing a hymn, even to pray for someone else or ask for something and believe from the Lord. It is called an act of faith.

We clearly see in the Bible in *verse 29* of *Mark 5,* that the woman with the issue of blood made a bold step of faith and walked through the protocol of apostles and disciples and squeezed herself to touch the garment of Jesus as an act of faith. Nowadays, Jesus gives us his messages in our midst by his messengers such as the pastors, evangelists, apostles, teachers, prophets and our fellow believers even in his holy Word (Bible); or through reading a witness book like this one you are reading right now.

Furthermore, it might be an altar call in your Church, or tele-evangelism or any congregation of the Bible believing Church. It might be a fellowship where the preacher might be convicted of a situation as the Lord might like to help you. Do not fear those onlookers or spectators or be distracted by the crowd. Just be bold and take a step of faith to move or walk forward to the altar and let the divine power of Jesus touch you, and fill you and make you whole again. It happens in many ways for instance; a preacher or a worship leader might ask the congregation to repeat after her or him with certain words, do it. It might be that he or she tells the congregation to stand and dance to a tune, do it. The Bible says that everything we do whether in word, deed or action let us do it in the name of the Lord Jesus, giving thanks to God the Father through him (by glorifying God). *(See Colossians; 3:17)* Be humble and do it as you believe faithfully for God to do something amazing and new in your life for his glory. That is when Jesus feels that you have touched him as it happened in bible in the scripture *of Mark 5:30* it says, *"At once Jesus realised that power or virtue had gone out of him. He turned around in the crowd and asked, 'who touched my clothes?'"*

I am of the opinion that an act of faith from a believer pleases God *(Hebrews 11:6);* that it quickens Jesus to realise that you are yearning and desiring his presence, because: *"In his presence, there is fullness of joy and pleasures forever more" (Psalm 16:10).* It is, in the same way, no one wants a lazy child who never grows up even in their 20s. If they cannot speak, then that is an abnormality, or if they cannot respect you when you arrive at home from a certain age, they are rude or out of hand, you do not want to give them precious things or go with them to dignified places. However, a well-behaved child who respects his or her parents makes them proud and they would like to display him or her to the entire world. That is what happens to Jesus and our God. When you trust, honour, obey and recognise Jesus, then God makes you a display of his glory by anointing you, healing you and giving you all your hearts' desires. *(Paraphrasing: John 16:23-24)*

Jesus saviour of the world, then will he love all?

By coming and saving the whole world, Jesus Christ demonstrated God's love, and the truth is: he is the love of God for humanity. Yes, he loves the entire world. *(Paraphrasing: John 3:16)* Due to the fall of the first man (Adam) in *Genesis 3;* all humanity and the entire world was short of the glory of God. Adam and Eve were cast out of the garden of God (Eden) from the presence of God, which was paradise on earth. Because of the love of God, he sent his only Son Jesus Christ to save us and restore us to our former glory through Salvation, by suffering, crucifixion and died on the cross at Calvary. On the third day, Jesus Christ rose again by the power of God and he is in heaven always interceding or pleading for us. Therefore, whosoever believes in Jesus Christ, their sins are forgiven (remission of sins) and receives love of God, grace of God; eternal life *(shall not perish but lives an everlasting life after this life in heaven).*

But there is an invitation to you as a person to invite Jesus into your life or heart and let him be your business and centre of focus and surrender to him. God is faithful; He gave us a choice that the word is in your reach; believe Jesus that he is the Son of God and that he died for you and saved you personally; repent of your sins and confess him as your Lord and saviour then you will be saved. *(Paraphrasing Romans 10:8-11)*

There would be a doubting person who might ask: how comes Jesus will manifest to only those who are born again? And those who invite Him and seek him with all their heart and not to the whole world yet he is the saviour of the entire world? The answer is in the word that Jesus told us in the book of John 14:23. *"Jesus answered and said to him: "If anyone loves me, he will keep my word; and my father will love him, and we (Father and Son-Jesus) will they come to him and make our home with him (by the power of Holy Spirit)".*

Let us pray this Prayer:

Holy Father God in heaven, in the mighty name of Jesus your Son; I pray that: even now as I am reading this inspirational book of the divine healing power of Jesus that touched the woman with the issue of blood and made her whole again. It will touch and heal me and forgive all my sins to give me faith and become a brand new creature. Amen.

Prayer is the key to success as we see all through in the book of *Mark 5:25-34;* we evidently find out that this woman was a prayerful person. She had fixed her heart in trusting Jesus Christ the Messiah. It takes a person with faith and faith is a character of prayerful people who regularly talks to God in daily devotions in the Word of God, in fasting and fellowships. That is why we see clearly that Jesus said to her, *"Daughter, your faith has healed you, go in peace."* *(Mark 5; 34)*

The Word of God is true and faithful. God has good plans for us we are encouraged to pray in the Word of God in *Jeremiah 29:11-13* it is written: "For I alone know the plans I have for you, plans of peace and not of disaster, to give you a future and hope. Then you will call upon me and go and pray to me, and I will listen to you. And you will seek me and find me, when you search for me with all your heart." *(Jeremiah 29:11-13).*

True worship: (humble, fear/reverence, trust, obey) in spirit and in truth.

Fearing God is the key to unlocking unanswered prayers. When you hear from God you do obey his voice and you do the extraordinary, God moves you on a higher status. For example, we read in the Bible in *Exodus 3* God made Moses into a god to pharaoh because, he heard from the God of Abraham, Isaac and Jacob; and this is the name of God as a memorial to all generations. Moses also led the Israelites from slavery of Egypt to freedom of Canaan the Promised

Land, because of the fear of God, and he maintained an intimate relationship with the LORD through his word. You can read a summarised life of Moses in *Acts 7;* while you get an insight of how the person who fears God is blessed as it is written in *Psalms 1*, you can read it and feel the power of God surge into your life.

Worshipping of God and trembling with fear before him is a sign of worship and Faith in God. Jesus had a dialogue with a non-Christian, who was just a religious who knew a hint of the Scriptures. And this is the Samaritan woman at a well, Jesus said to her; *"But the hour cometh and now is, when the true worshippers shall worship the father in spirit and in truth: for the father seeketh such to worship him. God is a Spirit: and they that worship him must worship him in spirit and in truth." (John 4:23)*

Prophet Isaiah was given this message to pass on to us and the Israelites at the time in the Book of *Isaiah 66:1-2 it is written, "Thus says the Lord: Heaven is my throne, and earth is my footstool. Where is the house that you will build me? And where is the place of my rest? For all those things my hand has made, and all those things exist," says the LORD. "But on this one will I look: on him who is poor (humble) and of a contrite spirit (fear me), and who trembles at my word (obey me)."*

In other words, worshipping God is a sign of faith. In our open verse, we see the woman trembling with fear and she told Jesus the whole truth. *(See mark 5:33)* her trembling with fear I repeat was a sign of worshipping Jesus! She reverenced our LORD with all her heart and she knew that Christ is a Holy Man and she had caused an abomination in the Jewish culture to come out of her enclosure, leave alone touching a Messiah! She put all her trust in Jesus to save her life and all the consequences of her bold faith. She didn't know if the crowd would stone her to death or to prosecute her; but I am of the opinion that she was convicted that on account of believing Christ Jesus as a merciful Saviour and kind Holy Man; she will be spared at his mercy. She only believed and put her faith in Jesus and she came out to worship him in order to glorify his name among the crowd. And this miracle still stands as a memorial until now.

I hope that this woman used to hear and read her Bible or Jewish Scriptures the Torah in her sick bed; where the Word of God that magnifies God among the crowd when he saves you from death and gives you life again, this is also my favourite scripture in *Psalm 116 from verse 1 to verses 6:*

"I love The LORD, because he has heard my voice and my supplications. Because he has inclined his ear to me, therefore, I will call upon him as long as I live. The pains of death surrounded me, and the pangs of sheol laid hold of me; I found trouble and sorrow. Then I called upon the name of the LORD: "O LORD, I implore you, deliver my soul!" Gracious is the LORD, and righteous; Yes, our God is merciful. The LORD preserves the simple; I was brought low, and he saved me." (NKJV Psalm 116:1-6)

God is pleased with people who worship him in spirit and in truth; Jesus said to the Samaritan woman at the well: *"But the hour is coming, and now is, when the true worshipers will worship the father in spirit and truth; for the father is seeking such to worship him. God is spirit, and those who worship him must worship in spirit and truth." (John 4:23-24).*

Reading the Word of God is also a sign of worshipping God: (Joshua 1:8)

By reading the Word of God is also a sign of worship and faith in God. The Lord commanded the children of Israel and all of us to read his Word, it is written; *"This book of Law shall not depart from your mouth, but you shall meditate in it day and night that you may observe to do according to all that is written in it. For then you will make your way prosperous, and then you will have good success. (Joshua 1:8)*

Just to give you some insights, I remember as a young person and a new believer; I asked the Holy Spirit the greatest teacher to teach me how to pray. I was led to read the book of Psalms as they are good in worshipping and praising God, while one of my mentors as a young believer also taught me that the book of Psalms are good. This is my personal experience, and I thought it would be good to share it with my readers. To emphasize strongly on this I boldly say that the Holy Spirit is the "Greatest Teacher" who can teach us all things and is the Spirit of truth who reveals all the truth about God. Ask him and pray to Jesus to fill you with the Holy Spirit and also to give you revelations of his Word, it is the work of the Holy Spirit. *(John 14:12-14)*

As you read the Word (Bible) you recite the scriptures and the Lord helps you by the power of the Holy Spirit to remember them, making you applying them in the circumstances you are going through and yield good results. The good results of reading the Word of God is mostly expressed in the book of Psalms chapter 119 verses 103 to 105 it is written: *"How sweet are your words to my taste! Sweeter than honey to my mouth! Through your precepts I get understanding; therefore, I hate every false way. Your word is a lamp to my feet and a light to my path. "(Psalm 119:103-105)*

The Truth:

Our Lord Jesus Christ calls attention to us believers who believe in him and he emphasizes that: *"if you continue in my Word, then you are my disciples indeed. And ye shall know the truth and the truth shall make you free."(John 8:31-32).* Jesus Christ is the truth. He explains himself in John 14:6: *"Jesus saith unto him, I am the way, the truth, and the life: no man cometh unto the Father, but by me."* Jesus goes deeper to explain that he is the truth of God, and the life of God, and the way to God the Father, no one can reach to the Father God except if he is transported through and by his Son Jesus Christ; this is well said evidently by Jesus himself: *"If ye had known me, ye should have known my Father also: and from henceforth ye know him, and have seen him." (John 14:7)*

Again we learn that Jesus Christ is the Word of God, as it is written: *In the beginning was the Word, and the Word was with God, and the Word was God (John 1:1).* This Holy Scripture unfolds what Jesus had told us in another explanation in John 14:7 in the above paragraph. For us to know that it is talking about Jesus the only begotten Son of God, the Bible gave us another explanation about the Word and the Truth, meaning Christ Jesus; for it is written: *"The **Word** of God became flesh and he dwelt among us, (and we beheld his glory, the glory as of the only begotten of the Father), full of grace and **truth."** (John 1:14)*

To emphasize more on this, the Word of God is the Truth and is received by faith. Jesus Christ was about to fulfil his mission on earth and he prayed for us to God Father, in his prayer he said: *"**Sanctify them through thy truth: thy Word is truth."** (John 17:17) When you go deeper again you will find that when you believe the Word of God in your heart; you become born again, and for this matter it is truly that the Word of God which is also the Truth is basically Jesus Christ. This can be sought in deep meaning from the

Bible it is written in the book of Romans 10: *"For with the heart man believeth unto righteousness; and with the mouth confession is made unto salvation. For the scripture saith, Whosoever believeth on him (Jesus) shall not be ashamed." (Romans 10:10-11)*

And hence Salvation is not qualifying only the Jews but also the gentiles (Romans 10:12) and God welcomes anyone who worships him in spirit and in truth; that is a heart issue now; where worship is directed by the truth rather than the ceremony. We see that in the Scriptures Jesus urged a Samaritan woman at the well and he told her that worshipping God will no longer be confined to one geographical location any more; but he emphasized that it is a heart issue where you have a personal relationship with God. Jesus explained to the Samaritan woman thus: *"Woman believe me, the hour cometh, when ye shall neither in this mountain, nor yet at Jerusalem, worship the Father. Ye worship ye know not what: we know what we worship: for salvation is of the Jews. But the hour cometh and now is, when the true worshippers shall worship the Father in spirit and in truth: for the Father seeketh such to worship him. God is a Spirit: and they that worship him must worship him in spirit and in truth" (John 4:21-23)*

The only way to have a personal relationship with God is through his Son Jesus Christ.

One touch of Jesus brings life, peace, joy and freedom: (John 8:36)

The Bible says that, him that the Son of God Jesus our Lord has set free is free indeed. And that we shall know the truth and the truth shall set us free. *(See John 8:31-36)* When one is sick and worried, you cannot have or feel peace; you are a prisoner and in bondage of fear of death or of the unknown, and worries or lack of confidence and self-esteem as you would not know what will come next! Again I will encourage you to completely depend on God for his Spirit to help you and comfort you and give you peace. *(John 14:13-18)*

But as soon as Christ Jesus touches me and you, that is a spark of divine power to transform us and makes us be filled with peace and freedom or liberty; hence healing. This is always followed by love, joy, peace, and righteousness of the Holy Ghost; and feelings of the strength in your body and mind or emotions. The woman with the issue of blood was set free, and Jesus restored her, and he said to her, *"Daughter, your faith has made you whole (well). Go in peace, and be healed of your affliction." (Mark 5:34)*

In other words, Jesus was affirming to her that you have been set loose and set free from the chains and shackles of the devil. Don't be anxious or worry again, be thankful, grateful and prayerful to God; the truth (Jesus Christ) has set you free; therefore, you are free and live your life in the peace of God that surpasses all understanding in your mind and heart unto the glory of God through Christ Jesus. *(See Philippians 4:6-7).*

Again and again, his word reminds us in *Psalm 147:3: "He heals the broken-hearted and binds up their wounds".* God furthermore says that *"The Lord sets prisoners free, The LORD gives sight to the blind, The LORD lifts those who are bowed down, and the LORD loves the righteous". (Psalm 146: 7-8)*

One thing for certain, is that one touch from the LORD is able to make me and you be spiced up and shine with him. Jesus is our righteousness; when he touches us, we become righteous! Come on now! That makes me remember how Jesus had made me shine before men as this woman after one touch from the Master our beloved LORD and Saviour. For it is written as Jesus said to me and you; *"You are the salt of this world. You are the light of the world. You are a city built on a hill that cannot be hidden; neither do men lit a candle or lamp and put it under the basket or bushel, but on a candlestick or lamp stand; and it gives light to all that are in the house. You are the light of this world, let your light so shine before men, so that they will see your good works and glorify our father in heaven through his Son Jesus." (Mathew 5:13-16)* I pray that this happens to you now in Jesus name.

Indeed this came to pass; as surely as Jesus touched this woman she had a privilege to testify among her family, relatives, neighbours, community and many others. So the LORD made her life to shine again before people. Even those who thought she would never make it again in her life! That is why I love Jesus! He did the same thing to me also; I am shining before all men to glorify God through Jesus Christ his Son for what a miracle of healing, deliverance, restoration and salvation to me. This big miracle brought glory to our Holy Father in heaven through the name of Jesus Christ his Son; right there even before the crowd. How great is our God, indeed he is worthy of the highest praises. Halleluiah!

"When Jesus says yes nobody can say no" is a song I enjoy to sing and confess many times! Jesus looked at her joy and faith and the fear of God in her heart and blessed her graciously; He did it again for me. He had already healed her in secret, but he needed to confirm the healing in verse 34(b); *"go in peace and be freed from your afflictions/suffering"*. Period; this woman and I will never be ill again. Jesus has sealed it with his Word and his Spirit. Bible says that the Word of God is living and powerful (Hebrews 4; 12a); furthermore it says that his word is true and faithful (Revelation 21:5)". And this had already happened to me as you will see in the next chapters as I testify about the miracle working power of the name of my Lord and Saviour and healer, Jesus Christ.

CHAPTER THREE

NEW BEGINNINGS

I would like to lay a foundation of the life as a born again Christian and how to keep the walk as a restored believer or revived believer or a new believer.

God makes everything new. Sister or brother in Christ, as you are reading this inspirational book, I would not know what you have been encountering in your life; but I am here to declare to you that this is your new beginnings, if you have renewed your faith in believing on Jesus! Believe me that our Lord can wipe away all your tears, heal you and even transform you and give you strength, and prosperity. Be encouraged as his Word tells us in *Revelation Chapters 21 from verses 3 to 7* as I quote:

"And I hear a loud voice from heaven saying; "Behold, the tabernacle of God is with men, and he will dwell with them, and they shall be his people. God himself will be with them and be their God. And God will wipe away every tear from their eyes; there shall be no more death, nor sorrow, nor crying. There shall be no more pain, for the former things have passed away." Then he who sat on the throne said, "Behold, I make all things new." And he said to me, "Write, for these words are true and

faithful." And he said to me, "it is done! I am the Alpha and the Omega, the beginning and the end. I will give of the fountain of the water of life freely to him who thirsts. He who overcomes shall inherit all things, and I will be his God and he shall be my son." (Revelation 21; 3-7)

Our God is the Alpha and Omega; whatever has a beginning has an end. God can put a stop to whatever sufferings you have. Just surrender all to God and give him your life, your sufferings, your heart, your mind, your dreams, your plans, your family, your business, your unemployment, your ministry, your marriage, and your job and let him mould them the way he wants. Let the will of God be done in all your endeavours, let it be all your now and inspirations, plans, aspirations and challenges.

I implore you to continue trusting God and lift up your hope as Jesus is our living hope! Do not lift up yourself in your effort; let the Lord lift you up. Always pray for God's will to be done in your life. I have been taught by the Holy Spirit to pray that God's will be done in my life; I learnt that from Jesus when he would pray. Do not fear anything because God did not give us a spirit of fear but of power, of love and of a sound mind. *(See 1Timothy 1:7)*

Believe that God will never leave you nor forsake you; he is always with you wherever you may be as he promised us in the book of Joshua. It is evident to us that even these Patriarchs and Prophets in the Bible were a hundred percent human, and they had to depend entirely on God in every step they had to take and every decision they had to make. Where they were discouraged, the Lord encouraged them such as in *Joshua 1:9*; The Lord said to Joshua who was the successor of Moses to lead the children of Israel and cross Jordan to the promised land of Canaan; *"Have I not commanded you? Be strong and of good courage; do not be afraid, nor be dismayed, for the LORD your God is with you wherever you go."*

In your new beginnings make sure you are always accustomed to prayer and seek God because those who diligently seek him will find him and he is the one who rewards us when we seek him. (*Hebrews 11:6 and Jeremiah 29:11-13*). Let us seek the face of the Lord.

It is imperative to read the word of God daily so that you are soaked in it; it increases your faith and blessings of God in our lives. This is a promise of God to the children of Israel as they were preparing to cross River Jordan into the Promised Land; "This book of Law shall not depart from your mouth, but you shall meditate in it day and night that you may observe to do according to all that is written in it. For then you will make your way prosperous, and then you will have good success." *(Joshua 1:8)* You are forgiven, and you are under the grace of God, therefore, no condemnation.

You are now living your life through the Spirit; this is a spiritual kind of life. It is written; *"Therefore, there is now no condemnation for those who are in Christ Jesus, because through Christ Jesus the law of the Spirit of life set me free from the law of sin and death". (Romans 8; 1-2)*

It is paramount to know now you are free and have already received the grace of God through faith, make sure you do not go back to your old sinful ways; don't sin again; have peace and feel freed and forgiven also forgive yourself plus others and love yourself plus others.

What I am trying to explain here is that: as a born-again Christian who has repented his or her sins and received Christ, after repenting your sins to Christ he has already forgiven you; so do yourself a favour and take it on by faith – believe as it is. You will not feel dizzy or have any physical difference, but it has already occurred spiritually, you are now a child of God. This is clearly illustrated in the word of God as it is written; "If we confess our sins, God is faithful and just and will forgive us our sins and purify us from all unrighteousness." *(1John 1:9)*

Make sure you do not start to condemn yourself, leave the past and look up to Christ our living hope, our future who will build you up as a brand new man or woman as we earlier saw in the scripture in (*1Corithians 5:17*).

This is emphasised more by saying that be consistent and let holiness be your value and virtue; do not sin anymore so as to keep your healing and your grace; as we lay more emphasis on this in the Word of God in *Romans 6:12-23 (read it).*

I am convinced that the woman in our opening verse (*Mark 5:25-34*) was built again by our LORD, as she allowed to receive healing in her body; mind spirit and soul. She stayed pure and did not sin again. I would like to glorify the Lord that despite all odds, I am a living testimony of Christ Jesus, who have saved me, and transformed me. And is taking me from glory to glory from victory to victory, even though at first I was just limping and learning gradually I am now more steps higher as the Lord teaches me how to live a godly way. It was not easy for me in the beginning, but the Lord has helped me, and forgives me my past mistakes even as Christian, and I am still learning. Therefore, I am encouraging you not to give up on yourself; you should surrender that habit to Jesus. And he will take care of you and break the bad habit in his mercy and grace; don't withdraw from fellowshipping thinking that you are judged, no one is judging you, we are all just learning from our Saviour, who is our helper in everything. Just go as you are if that gossiping habit has resisted, surrender it to the Lord, if that hatred or contention, or theft, or that habit of telling lies; Jesus will convict you anytime you are about to lie and replace it with the truth.

There are scenarios whereby some people get healed of some diseases, but they want to let negative emotions affect their mind and become a problem to others by being paranoid or thinking that they are less privileged. I want to let you know that it is very inappropriate to behave that way. If you are a Christian allow Jesus to do a good work which is new in your life; leave the past hurts, forgive all who offended you and release them; surrender to God wholly.

Stop dwelling on the past, don't drag the past hurts in your present and future. Leave old clothes/rugs and all pains of the early life in the past and say enough of that; It has wasted my time, and I am not taking it with me in my future anymore; it is an old junk of cloth which you are trying to patch on a new cloth! It is impossible; you can't maintain the bond, just say I want to live happily, and I will not carry my old negative emotions to the future because Jesus has given me a new wine and a new skin. I said that to myself; and I see it working for me that is why I am encouraging you now; I do not have to put my new wine in an old skin. We find this parable in the teachings of our Lord Jesus in the Book of (*Mathew chapter 9 verses 16 to 17 ;*) "*No one sews a patch of un-shrunk cloth on an old garment, for the patch will pull away from the garment, making the tear worse. Neither do men pour new wine into old wineskins. If they do, the skins will burst, the wine will run out and the wineskins will be ruined. No, they pour new wine into new wineskins, and both are preserved. (Matthew 9:16-17)*

Allow the Lord to work on you and make you whole again from the crown of your head to the sole of your feet, inside and outside your body (mind, spirit and soul). Otherwise; you will suffer consequences such as that even your closest relations will begin to avoid you or run away from you as you might be fond of finding every excuse to get upset about your past hurts. Let me be frank with you and point out that this does not only destroy and tarnish your image or character; it also affects your relationships whether at work, neighbours, family, Church and even as you travel. You might become so impossible and difficult to sit close to in the plane, bus, train or even bump into in a crowded place because you are too touchy and grumpy all the time! And if you don't pay close attention, this might even render you some other stress-related or psychological sicknesses and problems; for instance; being too critical of others and their progress, education, events, spouses, conversations, families, etc. You cannot afford to affirm anyone, or appreciate anyone not even yourself that people just tolerate you than enjoy your company.

I pray that this is not your portion, that you receive healing of inner wounds in Jesus name. Therefore make sure that you clothe yourself with the Full armour of God as the word of God tell us in this context that; *"Finally, be strong in the LORD and in his mighty power. Put on the full armour of God so that you can take your stand against the devil's schemes. For our struggle is not against flesh and blood, but against the rulers, against the authorities, against the powers of this dark world and against the spiritual forces of evil in heavenly realms. Therefore, put on the full armour of God, so that when the day of evil* come, (if you start to feel discouraged or think negatively of yourself and other people), you may be able to stand your ground, and after you have done everything to stand. Stand firm then, with the belt of truth buckled around your waist, with the breastplate of righteousness in place (chest); and with your feet fitted with the readiness that comes from the gospel of peace. In addition to all this, take up the shield of faith, with which you can extinguish all the flaming arrows of the evil one. Take the helmet of salvation (to cover your head); and the sword of the Spirit which is the word of God. And pray in the Spirit on all occasions with all kinds of prayers and requests. With this in mind, be alert and always keep on praying for all the saints."(Ephesians 6:10-18)

Apostle Paul was well aware of the fact that Christians who want to grow should not depend on the past, rather press forward toward a high mark of a high calling of God. (Philippians 3:12-16) says: "Not that I have already attained, or I am already perfected; but I press on, that I may lay hold of that for which Christ Jesus has also laid hold of me. Brethren, I do not count myself to have apprehended; but one thing I do, forgetting those things which are behind and reaching forward to those things which are ahead, I press toward the goal for the prize of the upward call of God in Christ Jesus. Therefore

*let us, as many as are mature, have this mind;
and if in anything you think otherwise, God will
reveal even this to you. Nevertheless, to the
degree that we have already attained, let us
walk by the same rule, let us be of the same
mind.")*

Helpful guidelines to help a Christian grow and live a miraculous life:

I have come with some practical guidance
which has helped me very well in my Christian
journey; though I didn't take a quick step in
some of them but the Lord helped me to get
there as much as I needed to and still going.

Water Baptism:

Make your decision to be immersed in water
which is referred to as water Baptism. It is
also referred to as repentance Baptism. It is
mostly illustrated its essentiality as Jesus our
model did it to fulfil all righteousness;
meaning that we must also do it as a walk of
righteousness; as we are being transformed
from sin into righteousness so that the
mission of Christian walk will start. This act of
Water Baptism is illustrated for us in the book
of *(Mathew chapters 3 ;)*

*"In those days John the Baptist came
preaching in the wilderness of Judea, and
saying, "Repent, for the Kingdom of heaven, is*

at hand"! For this is he who was spoken of the Prophet Isaiah, saying: The voice of one crying in the wilderness: 'Prepare the way of The Lord; make his paths straight.'" Now John himself was clothed in camel's hair, with a leather belt around his waist; and his food was locusts and wild honey. Then Jerusalem, all Judea and the entire region around the Jordan went out to him and were baptised by him in the Jordan, confessing their sins. But when he saw many of the Pharisees and Sadducees coming to his Baptism, he said to them, "Brood of vipers! Who warned you to flee from the wrath to come? Therefore bear fruits worthy of repentance, and do not think to say to yourselves, 'We have Abraham as our father, 'For I say to you that God is able to raise up children to Abraham from these stones. And even now the axe is laid to the root of the trees. Therefore every tree which does not bear good fruit is cut down and thrown into fire. I indeed baptize you with water unto repentance," (Math 3:1-10(a))

The reason to note its significance is that our Lord Jesus was also baptised by John the Baptist in river Jordan as it is written; "Then Jesus came from Galilee to John at the Jordan to be baptised by him. And John tried to prevent Him *saying, "I need to be baptised by you, and are you coming to me?"* But Jesus answered and said to him, "Permit it to be so now, for thus it is fitting for us to fulfil all righteousness." Then he allowed him." (*Mathew 3: 13-15*)

Desire to be filled by The Holy Spirit:

This is also referred to as the second birth. It is done by Jesus Christ whom John the Baptist who was Baptising in water immersion for repentance, John the Baptist said; *"I indeed baptise you with water unto repentance, but he who is coming after me is mightier than I, whose sandals I am not worthy to carry. He will baptise you with the Holy Spirit."* (*Matthew 3:11*)

The reason to note its significance is that our Lord Jesus was baptised with water and later on in the due process, he was filled with the Holy Spirit, and he is our model *(living example)*. We can clearly see that immediately Jesus was baptised, the revelation of *John the Baptist* and those around him changed; he even saw heaven opening and heard Father God speaking about his Son. We can read this in detail to clarify this further, it is written; "when he (Jesus) had been baptised, Jesus came up immediately from the water; and behold, the heavens were opened to him, and he saw the Spirit of God descending like a dove and alighting upon him. And suddenly a voice came from heaven, *saying, "This is my beloved Son, in whom I am well pleased."* *(Mathew 3:16-17)*

We know for sure that what Jesus demonstrated for us, we should follow it, as it is written that we should fix our eyes on Jesus Christ our Lord, who is the Author and the Finisher of our faith. (*See Hebrews 12:2)*

When one get the *Baptism of the Holy Spirit,* God fills the person with the power to do and have exceptional qualities. We read about the power of the Prophets, Kings, and Apostles plus other great men of God in the Bible who were used by God as they were filled with the Holy Spirit or Spirit of God.

Now my sister or brother in Christ, if you want to function well in the Kingdom of God; it is very imperative for you to yearn for the infill or the Baptism of the Holy Spirit. For example, after our Lord Jesus was baptised, he had the power to resist the devil, and he fasted for forty days and forty nights in the desert. Jesus had the power to overcome and resist the devil, and he fled from him *(James 4:7);* and Jesus was demonstrating to us to humble ourselves before God and this cures worldliness. Also to show to us that before we serve God, we need Baptism and in-fill of the Holy Spirit.

We see clearly in the Holy Scriptures that as soon as Jesus had been baptised in water and filled with the Holy Spirit, he was ready for a bigger mission; to overcome the devil and started to minister after coming from the wilderness. Jesus had the power of the Holy Spirit filled in him when he was led by the Spirit of God in the desert and Satan tried to tempt him three times, but Jesus overcame him. Jesus came out of the desert and straight away, he started his mission of saving lives on earth while he still lives and growing his ministry of the doctrine of apostles for three years. "From that time Jesus began to preach and to say, *"Repent, for the Kingdom of heaven is at hand."* It was the time when he called on the first disciples who were fishermen at the lake of Galilee. "And Jesus went about all Galilee, teaching in their synagogues, preaching the gospel of the Kingdom, and healing all kinds of sickness and all kinds of disease among the people. Then his fame went throughout all Syria; and they brought to him all sick people who were afflicted with various diseases and torments, and those who were demon-possessed, epileptics, and paralytics; and he healed them all. Great multitudes followed him from

Galilee, and from Decapolis, Jerusalem, and Judea and beyond the Jordan. (*Math 4)*

The Power of the Holy Spirit given to a believer:

Before *Acts 2,* the Lord appeared to the disciples and told them to wait for the Promise of God, the Holy Spirit as it is written; "And being assembled together with them, he commanded them not to depart from Jerusalem, but to wait for the Promise of the Father. *"Which",* he said, *"You have heard from me; for John truly baptised with water, but you shall be baptised with the Holy Spirit not many days from now". (Acts 1:4-5) "But you shall receive power when the Holy Spirit has come upon you; and you shall be witnesses to me in Jerusalem, and in all Judea and Samaria, and to the end of the earth." (Acts 1:8)*

There is an outpouring of the Holy Spirit that Jesus Christ gave to us who believe in him when we are saved. You can yearn and desire for it if you haven't automatically considered that you have received it. It can come to you like a rushing of the mighty wind or something very uncommon and extraordinary happens to you or start to get new revelations and understand the Word of God on a higher level. We can see this going on in full measure on the Day of Pentecost; I will paraphrase the book of *Acts 2; "On the day of Pentecost the Apostles and most of the disciples of Jesus were gathered and they were timid and had locked themselves in the upper room. But when the Holy Spirit came upon them like a rushing of a mighty wind, the whole place shook like an earthquake; they were all filled by tongues of fire each on their heads. This changed their mind-sets (no longer in fear/timid of Pharisees or death) and they were speaking boldly witnessing Jesus Christ who is the risen Lord; and on that same day, Apostle Simon Peter preached and three thousand (3000) people got saved." (Joel 2:28-29; Acts 2).* What a wonder our Master Jesus is; He is the one who saved me from my death bed and he still reigns and works and ever working.

The power of the Holy Spirit auctioned in us helps us to change us from an ordinary person into having supernatural power to become a changed man or woman, ready to be used as a vessel of honour by God in an extraordinary way in his Kingdom. I believe that the woman who was with the issue of blood, having been touched and saved and made whole by Jesus, was much filled with the power of God to speak boldly what the Lord has done. This was an act of witnessing our Lord Jesus Christ, the miracle worker and the *"Greatest"* man who ever walked on planet earth. It is the same reason why I have courage and boldness to testify about the healing and saving and delivering and restoration power of our Lord and my master Jesus Christ my friend who sticks closer than a brother in my life.

There are many examples of people who did extraordinary things, because of the unique power of God or the Holy Spirit in their lives as they had been chosen for particular tasks. I am convinced that the Lord has filled me with his Holy Spirit at a time like this to bless his people who are being ministered to by reading this inspirational and testimonial book.

We have more examples in the Bible of such individuals who were anointed and filled with the power of God for the work of God in the midst of the Israelites for our example to know and understand and believe. For example, Saul was just an ordinary handsome, tall youth, who was going about his father's business; but the moment Prophet Samuel anointed him; the Spirit of the Lord came upon him and he became a different man to be used by God. *(1Samuel 10:1-7)*

Does the above example and illustrations of the Baptism of the Holy Spirit sounding so similar to the directives that Jesus Christ our Lord gave to his disciples in *Acts1: 1-8?* Of course yes. We see that Saul got boldness to prophesy and he was filled with power to become the first King of Israel. Before his coronation day, Saul was told by Prophet Samuel to wait for seven days. Prophet Samuel was directed by God to tell Saul these words; *"You will go ahead of me to Gilgal, where I will meet you and offer burnt sacrifices and fellowship sacrifices. Wait there for seven days until I come and tell you what to do".* *(1Samuel 10:8)* King Saul became the first king of Israel.

Wait on the Lord

We have read in the above scriptures and illustrations that men of God were always given orders to wait and be told what to do; or wait on the Lord. The Apostles were told by Jesus in *Acts 1* to remain in Jerusalem and wait for the Lord, who would fill them with Power of the Holy Spirit.

People of higher level in Christianity or those who want more always wait on the Lord. *Psalm 37 verses 7 says;* "Patiently wait on the LORD and he will give you all your heart's desires." It is a procedure for anyone who wants to receive the Holy Spirit Baptism – you have to wait! Pray – sing – praise – worship – repent – praise and pray as you are waiting on him!

You see friends, the disciples in the upper room had spent 50 days, praying and waiting on the Lord! And they yielded to the Word of God as Jesus had already commanded them in *Acts 1: 4-8.*By doing this, Jesus wanted to tell us about the procedures of waiting on him to Baptise us with the gift of God *(The Promise) in Acts 1:4-8* he said, "don't leave Jerusalem, but wait for the gift I told you about, the gift my Father promised. John Baptised with water, but in a few days you will be baptised with the Holy Spirit." As we have seen earlier on, this promise was fulfilled in *Acts 2* on the Day of Pentecost. This experience was fulfilling what Jesus told them earlier on in *Acts 1:4-8;* and they became his witnesses. This was prophesied in Joel 2:28-29.

To give you some insights of my testimony, when the Lord touched me and healed me, he baptised me the following morning while I was praying and giving thanks to God for the gift of Salvation through Jesus Christ. It took me a couple of years to get baptised and when I was about to get baptised in water; I would hear the Lord speaking to my heart: *"Get baptised and I will send you (commission you or use you)."* For me this was it; I needed to be sent; to go into all nations and preach the gospel. It is the same way as Jesus had filled the disciples with the Holy Spirit for the first time and the Apostles were commissioned in *John 20:21;* "So Jesus said to them again, *"Peace to you! As the Father has sent Me, I also send you."*

For this reason, Jesus has commissioned us and it is the general authority of all Christians to go and preach the gospel and make disciples. Jesus said to his disciples, *"Go into the entire world and preach the gospel to every creature. He who believes and is baptized will be saved; but he who does not believe will be condemned. And these signs will follow those who believe; in my name they will cast out demons; they will speak with new tongues; they will take up serpents; and if they drink anything deadly, it will by no means hurt them; they will lay hands on the sick, and they will recover." Mark 16:15-18 (also read Math 28:19-20) Jesus is with us always until the end.*

In the context of my testimony, after Jesus had healed and saved me, I was still limping as I grew day by day. The Lord helped me, and I remember the day I yielded to the Holy Spirit and got baptized in my local Church Liberty (who hired a pool in another Baptist Church some few kilometres away in town). I do honor God for Apostle Lincoln Serwanga and his ministry. I was so overjoyed and felt at peace ten years on now.

My life has been totally transformed into a changed person and since that day I stand on the promises of God thus says: *"My soul does magnify the Lord, and my spirit has rejoiced in God my Saviour. For he has regarded the low estate of his handmaiden: for behold, from henceforth all generations shall call me blessed."(Luke 46-48).* From that day I received water Baptism, I believed that I am living according to *Proverbs 4:18 "but the path of the just is like the shining sun, that shines ever brighter unto the perfect day".* I am getting brighter and brighter moving from glory to glory from victory to victory in Jesus name, - Amen! God uses me more, and I hear from the Lord, and I walk in the divine supernatural provision of Jesus Christ; I haven't arrived yet, but I am so grateful for his mercies, and the grace of God is sufficient for me.

I can only say that a believer who has not received the baptism of the Holy Spirit is missing out on the fullness of our Lord! God gives a person who has received the Holy Spirit Baptism extraordinary revelations and favour and visions. It is clearly seen when Apostle Paul was in Corinth; at the time of persecuting the Christians. God spoke to him to work for God continually in that city, because, he was with him (God's presence or power – the Holy Spirit). Paul preached in a Synagogue, and the leader of the Synagogue was saved, and he was baptised. As I quote the Scriptures, *"And he departed from there and entered the house of a certain man named Justus, one who worshipped God, whose house was next door to the synagogue. Then Crispus, the ruler of the synagogue, believed in the Lord with his entire household. And many of the Corinthians, hearing, believed and were baptized. Now the Lord spoke to Paul in the night in a vision, "do not be afraid, but speak, and do not keep silent; for I am with you, and no one will attack you to hurt you; for I have many people in this city." (Acts 18:7-10)*

And on this note I will speak, and I will not be quiet, I will not fear, as God was with Apostle Paul, so he is with me. You are also free to join the vehicle of faith in witnessing for the Holy name of Master and Saviour Jesus Christ.

I would like to draw your attention that this kind of person who is convicted by God and receive Jesus Christ as his Lord and Saviour (Saved) and repent, get baptized with water and received the Holy Spirit is a functional believer. *(See in Acts 2, 10 and 18).* Allow me to draw some insight on types of believers.

CHAPTER FOUR

Are you a Stagnant or a Functional believer?

Some people might notice that some Christians pray and yet are not changed at all! These are the kind of believers the so-called stagnant believer yet they were baptized and speak in tongues. The word of God tells us that we are a new man. For example; one should stop lying, anger, stealing, obscene talks and malice, bitterness, hatred, contentions, perverts. And instead be kind to one another, if you used to steal now start to labour with your hands and give the needy; speak with grace from your mouth, forgiving one another, and we should not grieve the Holy Spirit. *(Ephesians 4:25-32)*

According to the word of God, one's heart must change. A person needs to change his or her mind-set; get proper transformation and allow the Lord and his word to touch you, and believe in his values and virtues of the Holy Spirit. God tells us that Jesus had the virtues (gifts) of the Holy Spirit. It is written: *"And the Spirit of the LORD shall rest upon him, the spirit of wisdom and understanding, the spirit of counsel and might, the spirit of knowledge and of the fear of the LORD; And shall make him of quick understanding in the fear of the LORD:*

and he shall not judge after the sight of his eyes, neither reprove after the hearing of their ears: But with righteousness shall he judge the poor." (Isaiah 11:2-4)

Change from your old values, some traditions are so superstitious and ungodly, drop them and adopt good godly Christian values; such as new Christian values of dropping that old boy or girl friend and living a celibacy life until you get married, even if some cultures do not value it, but it is a godly thing.

As I tell you now; I grew up in a polygamous family that is number one; though my Dad repented and God restored him later in his life before he passed away.

Concerning Evangelicals or born-again or Pentecostal belief and things; I had no model at all, the Lord used me to stand in the gap to be a model in my family for new family believers and our children, praise Jesus. My youth were not sweet because of an illness you would read on in the coming chapters. However, our God in his gracious and kindness had mercy on me by his grace, and Jesus Christ saved me and healed me instantly.

I tell people that I was a born-again young person who I would still want to catch up with my teens that I had missed. I started to go to discos like never before for a while. I would go to Watoto Church (KPC then) to see my Pastors Gary skinner, his wife and youth Pastor then Pr Chris Komagun and other ministers to pray for me as I was concerned I was not behaving to Christian standards since I used to go to night clubs with my brothers and ex-fiancé. But mostly I would cry to Jesus to help me because my body would do what my spirit hated so much – night clubs! This was a big concern for me, but I didn't know how to control myself except to pray and ask for forgiveness and also take the habit away from me! Brethren, we need to stop and examine ourselves and recognise our wrongs then seek help from the Lord as I did. Then, later on, the Lord convicted me of this sin, and I stopped instantly, my peers found me to be boring, but I said it's better to obey God than uniting myself with darkness and sin. However, I am not anymore a people pleaser I became a God pleaser and I pray it remains that way.

Jesus Christ restored me later on still in my youths that he convicted me to live celibately up to into an adult age (mature lady) when I got married a couple of years ago – Praise the Lord. Greatly I liked the idea, because; Jesus said to me that my body is his temple, and as I lived celibately without a boyfriend I would care much more about the things of the Lord more without distraction. *1Corinthians 6 and 7*, we will see below had worked for me when the Lord restored me! And I am so grateful for that gift, up to until one finds a suitable partner. When some people who knew me as a mature person heard me say in my new life as a restored Christian (Functional believer) that I was celibate, they would ask me until when? After all, It was the best experience at first. Therefore I said for when the Lord says I can get married. I surrendered my feelings and passions to Jesus to completely own me and control me and take over all my desires and aspirations. He would give me desire to get married, but not out of peer pressure, lust, passion, routine or convenience as before. I would like to inform ourselves that this is the way forward. Start to hold yourself now in the *21st Century* where it is a fashion to hang on to bogus relationships without appropriate marriage. It is wiser not involve yourself in sexual actions, because, I suffered the consequences as a young person for this ignorance, and I need to let someone know before it is too late!

Even if someone is engaged to you, abstain from sex, wait until you get married. It is a sin, and it defiles your body to indulge in any sexuality behaviours before marriage, and God and his Spirit are detestable to sin committed when knowingly. God teaches us that our bodies are His temple so we should use our bodies for his glory. As it is written; *"Now the body is not for sexual immorality but for the Lord, and the Lord for the body. And God both rose up the Lord and will also raise us up by his power. Do you not know that your bodies are members of Christ? Shall I then take the members of Christ and make them members of a harlot? Certainly not! Or do you not know that he who is joined to a harlot is one body with her? For the two he says shall become one flesh. But he who is joined to the Lord is one Spirit with him. Flee sexual immorality. Every sin that a man does is outside the body, but he who commits sexual immorality sins against his own body. Or do you not know that your body is the temple of the Holy Spirit who is in you, whom you have from God and you are not your own? For you were bought at a price (of the blood of Jesus when he died at the Cross at Calvary), therefore glorify God in your body and in your spirit, which are God's."* (1 Corinthians 6:13-20).

A functional believer always blesses the name of the Lord and the love of God anchors his or her heart that is to say; the person gets into a more intimate relationship with our Lord Jesus Christ. I can say that I have been enjoying this intimate relationship with our

Lord Jesus Christ since I lived celibately and my body became the temple of the Holy Spirit and it gets sweeter and stronger day by day. *(Proverbs 4; 18)*

With regards to our opening scripture in this book, the woman in *Mark 5:25-34* must have been baptised and got even more intimate with Jesus Christ by receiving the Holy Spirit. We see that she left changed and transformed; there is nowhere again in the scriptures does it say that she was sick again. She was transformed by the power of God and she kept on witnessing Jesus name to many in her family, community and life's circles. I reckon her transformation impacted many people who saw her and followed and supported the ministry of Jesus Christ in the early days of Christianity.

These are the things that happened to me when the Lord touched me and healed me and saved me and I became born-again.

Firstly, I changed my heart and the way I used to think (mind-set). I saw sin as something that was tarnishing my new life of Christianity- since I was restored again; though it might sometimes be gradual or instant, whichever way, I allowed the Lord to work on my character. My friends and circles changed as I yielded to Jesus Christ for more of his transformation to take place in me. I was consistent to live a celibate life and I would pray for all loopholes to be blocked by Jesus that I belong to him alone and my body is his temple, a temple of the Holy Spirit.

"Do you not know that your body is the temple of the Holy Spirit who is in you, whom you have from God and you are not your own? For you were bought at a price, therefore glorify God in your body and in your spirit, which are God's." *(1 Corinthians: 19-20)* I said no and denounced all superstitious beliefs and practices; that was instant; blessed be the name of the Lord Jesus Christ for the power of his Holy Spirit for conviction and standing firm in my new belief of Salvation. I was so bold and excited and still have the joy to share my experience of being a born-again with others to inspire them and evangelise the good news of the Kingdom of God. Having started with my family, neighbours, friends at college and the circle grew bigger as the Lord made me enter into my adulthood and as I entered into employment. The seed of Salvation has germinated in me and has brought forth new trees that have been fruitful and harvests in the vineyard of the Lord that most members of my family and close friends have been saved. All praise and honour go to God through Jesus Christ our Lord, Saviour and redeemer.

I still use the humanitarian message to present the gospel of Christ and his love to people; which is a very useful means to extend love to the hurting world. Especially orphans, widows, sick, needy, refugees, and elderly. I cannot boast; it is all done by the work of the grace of God that I received Salvation, not by my own works. (*See Ephesians 2:8-9*)

Renewed mind and attitude (The New Man)

The word of God in *Ephesians 4:22-24 says; "That you put off, concerning your former conduct, the old man which grows corrupt according to the deceitful lusts, and are renewed in the spirit of your mind, and that you put on the new man who was created according to God, in true righteousness and holiness."*

Stop acting like you used to act, have your mental and spiritual attitudes renewed and changed. I have been feeling the need to emphasise this as it is paramount in our lives as converted believers and Christians. Yes it is possible if you trust and obey Jesus Christ and yield to the Holy Spirit.

You should not let the devil dictate what you think or say (rebuke negative thoughts and confessions). But make up your mind according to the way God wants you to and think the way he thinks about you as it is written in *Jeremiah 29:11; "For I alone has the good plans about you, says The LORD. Plans to prosper you and bring you a future you hope for."* It would be better to stop contemplating on negative thoughts, also confess the Word of God and embrace positive thoughts, that is faith practiced right there.

It would be better if you occupy yourself by doing something at least to help yourself or others such as reading the scriptures, praying, fasting, working, doing your domestic chores, etc. Also serving in your Church or local community as a volunteer or giving a helping hand to your neighbour with her or their children or going away to the park or for a walk in the forest, jungle, or solace place or play music; gospel music would be the best to minister to you.

If you are negative, every morning the enemy would want to get your thoughts if grumpy. Be positive and say, I am going to have a good day today; even if you don't feel it, just act it and believe it as you said it. I also do this and it is practising real faith based on the word of

God; it works for me and I hope it will help you too.

Your thoughts affect your outlook. If you need a breakthrough, believe. Say and think 'I believe that my future is going to be better than my past. Take responsibility for your life. And I can hear someone is saying, 'but it is not my fault'!

Alright, I can understand that, but partner with God; He is able to fix it with you and you must allow him. I was there and kind of know what it takes to believe God and trust him for every step I take; I mean every single step I take. You know this life we live is not our own, it belongs to God, even the air we breathe is his Spirit and I do believe so. Therefore, let him have it back, surrender it to the creator Almighty God to do something good and new for you. So I didn't tell you to fly, but you can just limp, walk, believe, trust in God, and hold on to Jesus the Lord's Messiah who helps us and solves all our problems.

I would like to tell you a proverb one preacher said. One day a man went for a mountain climbing and he was nearly to the top of the mountain that he fell off in the night, he came tumbling down and he was lucky and got to the grip of hard rock. He called for his dear life saying: *"Is there anyone to help me?* It was very dark in the night and he thought he was holding on to a cliff many hundreds of metres away from the ground. He heard a voice saying: *"Yes there is God".* So the man holding on to dear life and breathless he replied: *"Ooh God, help me!!"* And God replied: *"It is alright son, just trust me, let go and drop down I am with you."* The young man just continued crying so bitterly and he was so fearful to let go and drop down, to surrender his life to God. So he stayed for long hours in agony holding on to the cliff. At dawn, as the daybreak was coming, he could see that he was very close to the ground. He only stretched his legs and he stood on the ground, he did not need to struggle all night in agony to fear to let go the cliff as God had told him; he was so ill and tired.

This story teaches us a moral lesson that some people would call to God for help and when he answers instantly and gives them instructions, they would not like to trust completely and obey in God or Jesus Christ or yield to the Holy Spirit. They do not want to surrender; they still want to live in agony and fear and uncertainty like the young man the mountain climber. This should stop. When I was a new believer, I would sing this song that taught me not to fear but trust in God; it goes like this: *"Jesus You are my firm foundation, in you, I can be secure......."* It was a prayer for me and I meant every word I would sing in prayer, even when I am feeling wobbly I trust God.

Therefore, you need to get going and spend time with God. It is not only to spend time with God but give God time. Stop working God around your schedules and start working your programs about God. This is what the Word of God in *Psalms 91-1* says: *"He who dwells in the secret place of the Most High; shall abide under the shadow of the Almighty."* Spend time with God; - you can hide for two minutes in the bathroom at work and speak to the Lord, come on brethren! You have got to fight for your life!

Now next is my personal encounters and testimony of Jesus healing and saving me in the next chapter, stay tuned and blessed as you continue to read on.

CHAPTER FIVE

MY TESTIMONY

"JESUS TOUCHED ME AND MADE ME WHOLE".

The lyrics of a song came to my mind as I was preparing to write this testimony;

"Shackled by a heavy burden,

Beneath a load of guilt and shame.

Then the hand of Jesus touched me,

And now I am no longer the same.

He touched me, yes he touched me;

And ooh the joy that flood my soul.

Something happened and now I know,

He touched me and made me whole."

What a glorious experience to be touched by the mighty handoff Jesus! Certainly after just one touch, I will never be the same again! By just one touch of the saviour and redeemer's hand, sickness leaves our bodies; we are transformed by renewing of our minds, and we are no longer slaves unto sin, yokes are destroyed as all my yokes were destroyed. Just by one touch of the Master's hand bondages and shackles of chain are broken as all my bondages were broken. By the mention of the name of Jesus; demons free and addictions are broken, characters are built as mine has been constructed. And there is a paradigm shift in our emotions, our desires, our spiritual statures and mental states. Our souls are healed as my soul was healed; because of the powerful and miraculous touch and Holy name of our Lord Jesus Christ (The Master's) hand. I will live to testify the goodness of the LORD in the land of the living. Amen.

I was brought up with caring and loving parents and had been taught values and good behaviours and morals.

I was living like any healthy, aspiring, vibrant and happy young person who was studying and had just been engaged to a young businessman in town.

Fate started that I had suffered an issue of blood for the past four years as a young person later on. It was a big test for my family and me that God turned it into a testimony as you will read on. I had tried all sorts of cures and treatments; whether traditional African herbs, traditional organics, Chinese, Scientific medicines, radiotherapy etc. But they were all in vain; nothing was there to seem to heal me at the time.

The hospitals were a familiar place around the year as I was used to be in and out regularly. Therefore, most doctors would tell my family to try traditional healing (witchcraft I would swallow many prescribed tablets or pills per day. I would drink pots upon pots of all sorts of traditional and organic herbs both raw and cooked! I was fed up with that situation and it wasn't an easy life for me as some of my age-mates.

However, I had refused to give up! Now I know that God has good plans for my life (*Jeremiah 29:11*) I always hoped that I would get better one day and become somebody. As time passed by I took responsibility for two infants, my younger brother and other relatives.

Having grown up in a devoted Catholic family; at home, my parents used to conduct two sessions of prayer per day. That is very early in the morning (6.00am) for 30 minutes and in the evening for two hours from 8 pm to 10 pm; Monday to Sunday, seven days a week. All throughout the year since I was a child this had been the family norm. I was raised by religious parents, and we were taught morals.

However, I pray for Salvation to continue to penetrate my family in Jesus name.

To be honest with you, sincerely from my childhood my Dad and Mum loved me so much I was one of the children who was over-protected among my siblings. Mostly Dad loved his daughters very well. I know they were both very concerned about my well-being, because, this was the third year of the sickness.

There was an incident that made me to desire to know and seek the love of God. It came over me during the evening devotions or prayers that my father was leading us that one night. And I think due to instabilities in the country and neighbouring countries at that time, he prayed for mother, all the big brothers and sisters in their order, relatives and all his farm house but I don't know why I did not hear him mention my name to pray for my sickness as he used to do it on a daily basis. It used to give me hope if I would be prayed for. I don't think that my Dad could have forgotten me, but it might be that because of the pain I was going through; I could hardly concentrate, and most of the time due to much medication I would doze off. I think I just missed it and I know that God makes all things work for my (our) good. *(Romans 8:28)*.

So when I didn't hear Dad pray for me in that night devotions, I got upset and I started to cry out desperately "how about me Dad? Don't I need prayers to get healed of this disease? Have you have forgotten to pray for me Dad? Do you still love me Dad? My Dad was a disciplinary man whom you could just not utter things anyhow; this time he kept quiet and felt so sorry for me! For the norm was that no one interrupts prayers; so he paused for a while and let me speak, when I had finished he continued to pray. The reason is that I was a very humble - well behaved and meek girl! I had never been acting like that in my life! In fact, I saw my Dad was very concerned and he thought that I had got into a crisis. I saw my Dad and my Mum were very sad that night!

Therefore, I went out of the house and I had sat on the balcony or veranda of our main house alone in the night weeping, because even all my young siblings, servants and porters, maids were inside for the evening or night devotional prayers – this is still the family norm and values. I could hear my Dad leading prayers in a very tearful voice! I also made my parents confused! But they remained crying for the Creator God to help me and them. I used to be scared of getting out at night on my own due to political instabilities in the country, but that particular time of the night I was very brave for some reason I could not explain. That is the night I knew that I was a grown up person; I needed to fight and vend for my dear life, to grow up and seek the face of the Lord to heal me. Literally I did not know that the Lord wanted to use me as a vessel of honour in his Kingdom of heaven, after a through work on me with a brand new life in Christ Jesus. (Psalms 126).

During my sickness I asked myself a question *"who loves me that I can feel it in this physical and emotional pain and heal me, and where can I go now to be healed?"* While I got out in the night and I sat on the veranda all by myself it was moonlight; in that solace and what seemed a very lonely night! My heart and thoughts were pondering on God alone and how amazing he is. I yearned to know him and to feel his love, comfort, joy, peace, glory (to remove pain and reproach or shame from me) and heal me. I looked at the bright moonlight and shining stars in the sky, then I thought about the whole universe and the wonder of God's power for sustaining the entire universe. I said: "God, you hold these entire big galaxies in the universe, help me Father! Please help me God!" I had learnt to pray and know the basics of Christianity from my Old Catholic religion. And I also knew that God is our Holy Father, the Creator of heaven, and earth. I knew that Jesus Christ is the Son of God and he came to save us all from our sins and I knew about the Holy Spirit. I had learnt the Trinity but I wanted to feel connected and needed to know which religion will connect me to God. Do you know that later on I found my prayer for that night is in Bible in *Psalms 91:1 it says: "He that dwells in the secret place of the Most High shall abide under the shadow of the Almighty." (Psalms 91).* I also repented to God right there for interrupting the prayers and being naughty to my Dad for the first and last time in my life. I looked up and I felt very empty and hopeless, rejected, and unloved at that only brief one moment in my life though I was always confident that I am loved; pain had gone to my nerves and it had broken my confidence! I thank God for it because it made me realise that I need to seek God's love, I was seeking human sympathy which gains nothing if you are not in the Lord. My parents loved me to bits and as far as I knew they could do anything for us their children and they would assure us daily, but in just a brief moment of not sucking the love, I was throwing tantrums.

I apologised to my Dad and Mum and everyone and life went on as usual. While this caused me more consequences that my parents increasingly became overly-protective of me, even with regards to my siblings. I thank them so much for that love, care and protection. However, the solution was in the hands of God my Creator, this was not a human intervention but Jesus Christ had to intervene divinely and touch me to give me life. I had just sensed it within my heart at the balcony in the night just alone that God needed to intervene on a higher level for me to get healed, but I had needed to seek his face as the one who created me. What the enemy had purposed for evil, the Lord has turned it into good for me. Even if one is taunted and intimidated by life's trials and tribulations, God will always come through and save you and me. (James 1:2-3) I want you to know that Salvation is personal no one can get it for you, or have mercy on you. It will come in packages and parcels labelled only with your name on it and no one will be able to receive it for you. It is a unique and personal relationship with Jesus Christ that is beyond measure and human understanding; whatever it takes, you will receive Jesus. He will create a way where there is no way as he did it for me and the experience is awesome and amazing to live close to his heart as a child of God living in Christ Jesus by being saved.

I am so grateful for loving parents and I do not take their love for us children for granted, thanks be to God, it is a wonderful thing in life. However, when you do not have Jesus, parental love, or relations love does not satisfy. I still felt empty, ill and broken. I was unwell almost dying, helplessly before the eyes of my loving parents and siblings. Moreover they had also gone into stress for their unwell daughter and sister! Around the neighbourhoods we were the laughing stock because we were prayerful Catholics and make noise to the neighbours in night devotions; but in the family, the most beloved daughter was unwell. It was a kind of disgrace and reproach to me and my family; hence my parents had felt defeated at that time, but no more now, glory is to Jesus Christ who touched me and made me whole again, I am here to testify. Praise God Almighty Abba Father for his grace that saved a wretch like me. Amen.

Once upon a time one neighbour came and told my mother that she is a foolish woman for not taking me to witchcraft to heal me. I was there when my mother replied her; "I am not God to give life! God who gave me my daughter knows it all and I will trust God to help me and heal her. "She then sobbed, and the woman left.

In all of this struggle and pain, God knows us. This is the time God gave me to hunger and thirst for righteousness truth and love. I turned to all sorts of things to try to know God and his love for humans, especially for me.

The only thing I thought in my heart that if I quench this thirst for this kind of love of God, He will be able to make me feel better and heal me! Throughout all this for a couple of months, since the evening devotions incident, I started to develop these questions:

1.   Who loves me too much that I can feel it?

2.   Is Jesus Christ for Moslems or Christians?

3.   What is the Truth?

4.   Who am I?

I started to do research on my own by starting to listen to gospel music in our native language and it could give me a fix for a while.

Then every Fridays I could secretly tune into Friday Islam prayers on our local radio; and asking some Muslims why don't you eat pork? Did God forbid it? Is it a sin to eat pork? And can't I keep dogs? How about if I live in a home where there are pigs and dogs? Because my family own a country home so we live in a farm house with a variety of animals and poultry and gardens. I was asking some silly questions to know the truth, but I was looking answers from inappropriate and wrong channels or sources.

By doing all this I was questioning myself many times in my heart and mind: "Who loves me? And what is the right true and holy religion to worship the only and holy true God of heaven so I will have secured to go to heaven? I want to know if anyone really loves me and is not angry or ashamed or frustrated that I am going through this pain and shame; because even my fiancée who used to love me, at that time had abandoned me and his family had told him not to have any contact with me anymore! I was so lonely and my heart had been broken. Even though my parents and siblings would comfort me with their too much love, gifts, support, driving me to places, very comforting words, looking after me, hiring a maid for me, but I was in too much pain, though it made a difference, thanks be to God for all his grace that he gave me and my family through all this difficulty times.

Even though my parents and siblings used it as a song to always express their love in words and actions, so much that I know how to be loved by family because I grew up experiencing it. However at that point I wasn't feeling a deep sense of loneliness, but much rather despair, emptiness and pain because I had allowed the rejection and shame of my fiancé and his family and some spiteful relatives and locals to occupy my mind; because I would always be mocked by spiteful people with all their negativity. Let me tell you friends who are reading my testimony; when you are in trouble there are wicked people who would enjoy your struggles and even pretend to visit you or sympathise with you but inside they would be laughing even cursing. God warns us of such people in Ezekiel 33:31. However, there are also many good people out there who would mean good to you and pray for you and sympathise with you. Thanks be to God who strengthened me and my family to overcome and gave me victory by healing and saving me. I am like the woman in Mark 5:25-34. And I believe that I am a living epistle of Christ Jesus, I am a living testimony of the miracle healing power of Jesus Christ as you read on.

I said earlier on I was asking God questions, so my question number two was "God please tell me if Jesus Christ is for Christians or Moslems, what is the right religion should I follow in holiness and heal me? Is it Muslims or Christianity?

To make matters even worse; I had earlier on got engaged to a fiancé at the time who was a non-practising Moslem, but he would follow me to Catholic Church every Sunday because the norm of my family is that he must convert to Christianity if he was willing to marry me and he had agreed. He would tell you about their religion; most of the things that show that women are like a second-hand citizen; which seemed abnormal to me from the way I was raised as a Christian in the Catholic religion - we are all one in Christ as I was told and learnt from an early age.

Despite on the radio, it all sounded very unrealistic about women, I heard that they sit separately in prayers. I heard on the radio that we shared Abraham and I didn't understand the rest of the details.

Again I had earlier on said that the third question that was bothering me in my heart and mind was; "what is the truth?"

One day, I had a thought which dropped in my heart and mind while I was lying on my bed. I remember this question that popped in my spirit so sweetly it said, "Why don't you read the Holy Bible and find out the truth? I said I will read it when I get better.

After a couple of months listening to the gospel music such as: - Calvary Cross Choir, the Escatos Brides, and Pastor Simeon Kayiwa's Church hymns; also my Dad had tapes of Gospel hymns which were useful to my hearing. Perhaps some of my readers who have ever been to Uganda - East Africa might have heard of some of the hymns in those days of the 1990s. And the song I had registered more was; *"Touch now you sinner on the holy garment of Jesus, who will heal you where you are."(drawn from Mark 5:25-34 and John 3:)* It was such a kind of prayer for me.

Later on I headed to listen to midnight Christian Prayers every night and I felt at ease a bit, so I devoted to that for a while.

Meanwhile, I was still asking myself; *"what is the truth?"* Again the thought came into my heart and it said: Why don't you read the Bible and find the truth yourself?" I yielded to that thought then agreed; and so I started to read my Good News Children's Bible which my Dad had bought me (9 years ago) while I was finishing my primary school and joined the Catholic Convent in Secondary school aspiring to become a nun, but left, though this time I was in and out of college.

I read the whole Bible from Genesis to Revelation. Sincerely I really enjoyed the Old Testament as it was narrative, but I was more fascinated by the names. I found out that most of the Old Testament names sound middle-eastern, Hebrew or Arabic and the New

Testament names sounded Christian. I kind of got confused like any young person who was trying to find my identity. I had come to that youthful stage where you just don't tell a youth something, but they need to find out and get their Identity or their own experience. All this is The Lord's doing as the Bible says that *"It is good for me that I have been afflicted, that I may learn your statutes" (Psalm 119:71).* From my childhood, I used to be scared of hell, and every one of my siblings used to know that as a joke in the family; my Mum would tell me she prays that I should remain that way. I am still scared of it even at this point. I knew that Heaven is rewarded by God to righteous people, and hell as a punishment to wicked people; but I had got to a point of not distinguishing which religion to give in my faith: - Christian or Islam was my dividing line then.

I enjoyed reading the Bible but didn't remember much, though the word of the Lord was transforming me but I was only concerned with names. I didn't know that the invisible power and things are greater than the visible things. But God did well to me in his Word as I paraphrase in the Bible it says that the word of God is living and powerful; sharper than a double-edged sword, penetrating even in joints and bone marrows, dividing spirit and soul asunder; knowing all intents of men and nothing in all creation can be hidden from God. (*Hebrews 4:12-13*). Despite the human way of understanding; I had no revelation, because I had not become born again and not filled by the Holy Spirit so I did not understand anything into the book of Revelation. I was even much more scared of reading some verses narrating about creatures with many heads! But to God be the glory that since I became born again and Spirit filled Christian and child of God; the Holy Spirit supplied me with revelations.

As I mentioned earlier, I was confused about the Bible names in the Old Testament. One of the people whom I used to confide in and very closest friend is my sweet mother because I grew up in a very close relationship with her. Therefore; I again went back to ask her my troubled experience as I would always do and thanks to her that she mentored me well and she used to give me very meaningful answers, except this one, left her daunting. Then I asked my mother a question, *"Mama is Jesus Christ a Moslem or a Christian?"* My mum replied to me in tears; *"Oh God, please show and reveal your confused child the truth so that she don't get lost."* She then prayed; "Please Lord! Look at the pain and affliction of your child! Please, Lord, may you help her now". I also sobbed with her, because; my mum is a very soft humble - loving and kind lady; but I understood her prayer and her deep sense of concern though I needed to know God and the right faith to worship him and this was a matter of urgency and concern for me at that point. Lord bless my mother.

My mother gave me an answer in the form of prayer with her tears rolling down her cheeks; I was as well sobbing feeling a sense of yearning for the truth. Then I asked her; *"Mama you cry because you hate Muslims?"* Mum wisely replied to me: "God will show you the right way and truth." She again continued; "before you were born God gave me a name Christina for you and while I was still in the hospital after labour, that is the same name that your Dad named you and that name is in Christ Jesus, you belong to Christ." I remembered that most of the times my Dad used to call me in our language: "The anointed one of Christ.

When she finished her wise utterances of a Virtuous Woman *(Proverbs 31:10-31);* I felt very remorseful and kind of my heart melted, and softened, yet there was a kind of painful experience, but sincerely this touched my heart and I didn't know why? My Mama's wise answer gave me hope to know that I belonged to a holy person like Christ. I was always being called Christina the anointed of Christ by both my Dad and Mama since all my life but I had overlooked these good utterances on my life as the enemy was disturbing me, not anymore Jesus Christ is in control now.

Anyway, everything has its time and God's timing is the best and it was at that point. Thanks be to God for a mother like mine, who encouraged me that I belonged to Christ Jesus as she made me remember all my childhood experiences and at this point, I felt I belonged to Christ Jesus but I needed to get closer in a way I was not sure how; because where I was, it was not enough for me to feel his presence. I had marks of Christ written all over my life and I thought I needed to know God and Christ deeply. I had not become born again yet, and I was still suffering with the issue of blood.

I was sure that the Bible is the Holy Book and the Word of God. Therefore, I trusted God to show me the way, truth and life; so I stopped doubting if Jesus was for Christians after speaking to my mum, and then I made up my mind to look for him and know the truth. *"Jesus said, if you abide in my Word, you are my disciples indeed. And you shall know the truth and the truth shall set you free." (John 8:31-32)*

So for the second time again, *"I have decided to follow Jesus no turning back no turning back"* was added to my everyday songs at that moment and find out about Jesus Christ. I made it a point for the second time in a year; to continue reading the New Testament of my childhood Bible that my lovely Dad had bought me nine years ago when I was in my upper primary as I wanted to become a Catholic Nun, but left the convent later on in Senior secondary school. I would sing these three songs many times a day which goes; *"Jesus to remember you is the joy of my heart, but most of all anything I want to be closer to you."* The next one was *"I have decided to follow Jesus no turning back no turning back".* And the third one was; *"Touch now you sinner on the holy garment of Jesus, who will heal you where you are."* That was a kind of prayer for me for a long time as I was yearning for healing while continuing to read the Bible seeking to know Jesus Christ deeply.

At that time I did not know how to pray, like Evangelicals and I was not born again yet, so these songs turned into a prayer pattern for me and I knew the repetitive prayers of my former faith – the Catholic faith such as The Lord's Prayer, The Credo: *"I believe in God"* and the Rosary and reciting the Ten commandments. I was still ill, but I had gained more hope now to follow Jesus Christ only as The LORD of Christians and I hanged on there that I was glad I got my Jesus Christ back or he got me back on the right track (In the way, life and Truth). I loved to be a Christian, as I grew up in the Catholic Church being taught that Christianity is the only faith of truth and I believed it even more by this time than before. So I needed to build on this, and the love I always had for Christ since my childhood prompted me to ask who is this man who died for all the people, for all of us? I would ask my mother, that what did Jesus do to be crucified naked and humiliated? She would say to me that it is because of our sins and his love for us. I was young but now I had become a youth of an understanding age; so I wanted to know which sins have I committed, and everyone? Was this the reason that I was ill? I was taught of the fall of Adam and Eve, as a child and during my Holy Communion and confirmation sacraments; in Church, also at home in the mysteries of joy or sorrow or glory in the Rosary -always narrating that is why Jesus came to redeem and save us. I was reading the New Testament, all this started to make sense, however, I was still ill with bleeding problems but could have some gaps of relief though very unwell, only that I gained hope that at least I have got my Jesus back I am a Christian. Here I was a typical religious young person.

As I mentioned the reason I read the New Testament again is to get to know Christ Jesus in detail and what does the Bible say or God says about him. I also continued to listen to the local language gospel music and even bought more tapes. That year that I devoted to reading my Bible and listen to gospel music, my big sibling also became born-again. Whenever I visited my big siblings house brethrens would pray for me, I would agree to confess to receiving Christ as my Lord and Saviour but didn't mean it and I would go back to my old ways. I would see them all pray for me and cry with me, but I would think that they were very kind people. I would instead pull out my Rosary as they are praying for me and I pray it as well, saying to them that it is all prayers sometimes; this was hardening my heart.

Gradually, my heart softened and pain was on my nerve, that as I read the Bible (New Testament), the more my heart softened towards the things of the Spirit like born-again prayers and the preaching, though I didn't recognize that there was a change that sank in me, I would just live my life; but I believe every one of the believers were watering the seed in me by prayers and the Word of God I read to germinate and bear fruits of faith and I thank God for every believer who prayed and preached for me as a youth in my days of trouble and agony that ceased.

If I would feel a little bit better and go to work in my old school, there was a Born-again Church nearby and an occasional crusade in a national stadium near my college; so I would feel encouraged to pass by and listen and watch people testify that they were healed but I was adamant to join in to pray. The interest in listening or watching to the Word of God preached grew and I would also see people who are testifying of being healed. You know my heart was still in unbelief about miracles performed by Jesus Christ that I was so ignorant and would think that they had staged or performed them as many ignorant unbelievers or religious people might still think today. Pastors and Evangelists would make an altar call, but as young and as ill as I was, I did not come out to get saved. I even didn't know what process to go through to become a born-again; I was so ignorant that you must believe in your heart and confess with your lips. I felt like It was a thing for sinners who must tell all their sins in confession as I watched some people would do in public places -in buses and along marketplaces. Here I was a sinner and denying myself freedom from Christ for fear of shame yet I was being shameful every day because of the blood issue, this was bondage of sin. Thank God for salvation in Christ Jesus that it is all over now. And I am a candidate for the spreading of the Good News wherever I am in the world to all creatures.

The thing is; I would finish crusades or listening and reading the Bible or coming from the Catholic Church and praying the rosary; and guess what I would do because I was so hard-hearted that I would still continue to do traditional rituals, drink the traditional herbs, clays, medications, in and out of the hospitals, and unwell.

One day I had come from Mombasa Kenya on a vacation, and I passed my elder sibling's house. I had fallen unwell in Kenya with malaria and it was so bad, though I had a break from the bleeding for a few months. So when I went into the house I was greeted and to reading me *Isaiah 46.* The explanation to me was that I had a luggage and baggage that I needed to throw away and let Jesus take them away from me. Also, that these traditions of witchcraft or idols and all the stuff that I was carrying was like a tired animal; I should look on to the God of Jacob and God of Israel. My elder sibling suggested to me that we should join hands to pray for our family to get saved and we did. Since then I started to think of my Dad as Jacob and our family as the house of Jacob from this Holy

Scripture until now. However, the Word in
Isaiah 46 got to my grip, and it touched my
heart; and most visits to my big sibling turned
into a Bible study about this Word of God in
Isaiah 46 that had captured my heart, it
convicted me that I was a sinner and my
entire family and all human beings who are
not royal to God; therefore I would meditate
upon some of the Words during my own free
time at home as I quote;

*"Bel bows down, Nebo stoops; their idols
were on the beasts and on the cattle. Your
carriages were heavily loaded, a burden to the
weary beast. They stoop, they bow down
together; they could not deliver the burden, but
have they gone into captivity. Listen to me, O
house of Jacob, And all the remnant of the
house of Israel, who have been carried from the
womb: (these reminded me of what my mother
told me that Jesus Knew me and gave me a
name of Christina from her womb). Even to
your old age, I am he, and even to grey hairs I
will carry you! (I thought that even I can grow
old because I thought I would die, this word of
God brought me so much hope: Jesus is my
living hope)! I have made and I will bear; even I
will carry, and will deliver you. To whom will
you liken me, and make me equal (I was taught
as a kid that God is Almighty so it was so true
and a big revelation for me as I feared God)
and compare me, that we should be alike?"*

(*Isaiah 46:1-5* you can continue to read the whole chapter *of Isaiah 46*)

Though I was still weak the Lord is always strong, so through all my weaknesses the Lord was strong; ready to be patient with me and take me slowly by slowly, Jesus holding my hand as I was limping towards his Salvation – step by step forward.

You remember that earlier on I had mentioned that I was in the process of reading the Bible New Testament. I enjoyed other Chapters of the New Testament but I couldn't understand the book of Revelation.

I was so ill emotionally, that I would fear anything that mentioned death, and I had too much fear. I found the book of revelation terrifying to read a creature with so many heads etc. And reading about people going out of their bodies was so scaring to me; having not accepted the Lord yet in my life. So I had no spirit of revelation in me then, but not anymore, thanks be to God for saving me.

The year that I was redeemed

In the fourth year of my sickness, I was convicted to read my Bible from Genesis to Revelation again for the third time. I felt a sense of reconnection with my Christian Faith again, but I had not yet given my life to Christ Jesus as my personal Lord and Saviour to become a born-again.

I had completely cut off listening to Islam channels and switched on listening to gospel music quite a lot, almost all the time, day and night! I would tell my family that gospel music makes me rest and gives me peace of mind and they would agree with me. The fear of God increased in me.

I continued to tune into the Christian local radio midnight prayer hour to get prepared for my night's sleep.

I had a new venture of a local Television Christian Broadcasting that was delivered every Sunday at that time; literary called *"Seventh-day Adventist Programme or Hour"*. This is where all sorts of preachers would preach and I used to gaze but never used to listen what they were preaching; my emotions were getting better though the physical health was still at stake.

You remember that the fourth question that was bothering me was identity: Who am I?

My agony was a concern for every member of my family especially my parents and siblings; they could all do their best to help me feel better. May The Lord bless all of them, although right now my Dad and two of my big brothers went to be with the Lord. (R.I.P)

I had visited Catholic priests who gave natural herbs in Uganda. Additionally, my Dad then got me herbs from people who said they had seen a vision, but it was still in vain.

 Then my elder sibling who became a born again Christian took, me to a born-again Christian lady to pray for me and I did not hesitate to go most especially since I had started to read the Holy Bible I felt that there is real power in prayer, however I was still asking if Jesus or god loves me thought it was obvious now that Jesus Christ is for Christians. Actually, I had not paid any attention to the word of God! Because everywhere it is written that Jesus loves me! The reason is because I had not embraced his grace and loving power, I was ignorant like many of others now and I was so far away! God says; "draw near as I draw closer". And my prayer is that you get to know God that you don't perish as the Bible says; *"My people perish because of lack of knowledge"*. I soften to be prayed for by evangelicals; yet I would always pull out my Rosary because to me it was all prayers and I was thinking I was sticking guns to my old Catholic faith.

While I am still continuing with my testimony, I would like to give someone a piece of advice. Doubting is not good and God does not get pleased with unbelief, it doubts; because I was still not sure if Jesus Christ could touch me and reveal his power. You know why? Because I did not believe in my heart, I was using my logical mind and human effort. The truth is that it is by the grace of God that we are saved through faith; it is not by our works. Fortunately, Jesus needs our hearts and I am a hundred percent that my heart belongs to Him now! Do not think it through and reason his ability to heal or touch you or save you, don't use human effort mind-set or wisdom, just use your heart by believing and have faith to be humble! I know and understand that I suffered all these years because, I had hardened my heart, and nevertheless the Lord is merciful and gracious that he helped me believe with my heart and touched me, save me and made me whole again by his grace forever! Therefore I implore you my sister and brother do not harden your heart; soften it and go to Jesus he will see you through whatever you are troubled with he has the solution and comfort. Jesus Christ is the Lord's Messiah: the solution to all problems.

When my elder sibling took me with another family member to a Christian lady's house for prayers, I was dressed like a modern teen of the 1990s generation; in my skimpy miniskirts high heels - despite my illness. The first time she saw us she said: "you must repent or you will die". I was so scared, and I told my sibling, "did you bring me here to be cursed by this woman please take me out of here". You know what, inside of me I got concerned about my life, and she prayed for us and we left. (But no more death Jesus gave me abundant life and I have it more abundantly, Praise God.) I again re-examined my life and was repenting. After a while, I followed my elder sibling voluntarily and we went only two of us. The born-again lady prayed for me and she told me that Jesus loves me. I asked her what she meant. And how did she know? She said to me that Jesus will heal me if I accept him as my Lord and saviour. As I had a Catholic background, and I had been in a convent – literally to become a nun, I told her that I was already a Christian. I had my rosary and I felt a bit uncomfortable for her to tell me not to pray the rosary. But the Christian lady remained calm. They were other Christian's mostly dignified males in her house; later on, I learnt that they were also Pastors and they all prayed for me and they prophesied to me. They prophesied that the Lord chose me that I am his Prophetess and he will use me mightily. What? I said to my sibling in our language, "what kind of words are these?" The reason I was troubled was that they didn't know our language but prayed in English and said God chose me I am his Prophetess. In my language, prophetess is translated as the fortune teller, a term mostly used by superstitious or witchcraft people and I was very angry with witchdoctors and their practices of lies, wickedness and duping our money! But my elder sibling said to me that this is in a godly context and it is a godly calling that is a special divine gift from God in my life, *"You are blessed"*. This was so interesting for me with this new faith of evangelicals or born-again Christians I had just started to explore. Because; In my then current Catholic Church, there were no living prophets I knew of; except the ones that are written about in the Bible like Prophet Elijah, Prophet Isaiah; Prophet Jeremiah and so on. I thought to myself: just like that, for free, I was used to the normal ways of qualifying to serve God; that you have to go to seminary or convent and be ordained as a Catechist, Nun or a Catholic priest to serve God; so this was exciting! And kind of felt very liberating and interesting as I thought I always wanted to serve God and I thought my opportunity was gone since I had left the convent to become a nun; though my mum used to remind me more often that I can serve God wherever I am in many ways here now it had come to me sensibly. There was this kind of light at the end of the tunnel called *"hope"* right there; but I didn't know what for as I knew I could not become a nun again, but knowing that God has revealed something good about my life to serve him, yet I knew I was not worthy was a great news! Also to hear again that Jesus loves me after being rebuked was so liberating. Just because we don't see anything doesn't mean that God is not working is what I learnt.

The Pastors took the time to tell me and explain to me the meaning of Prophetess in English language and people that God used in that prophetic office. I knew the renowned Prophets Moses, Isaiah and Jeremiah. But I didn't know at that time how they knew that God will use me. Listen, people, how could this be! I pondered on this for many times and one of the dignified men (Pastors) said to me childhood experiences and encounters that I had never ever told anyone, you know why because I did not know how to express myself to tell my parents. They told me that Jesus knew me before in my mother's womb and he wonderfully and fearfully created me and chose me to be his servant a prophetess unto nations. I pondered on these things in my heart. *(Psalm 139: 1-14/Jeremiah 1:5).* I thought people have called me nick-names and doctors scared me of this illness, but these born again Christians were telling me words of hope, faith, encouragement, healing and love? These must be good people and a good religion, but it has to be God himself to show me the truth. Later on I found out that born-again is not a religion, but a personal relationship with Jesus Christ as your Lord and Saviour.

People of God, I want you to know that God loves us and he knows us, even before we accept Jesus! The Word of God is true that says that: *"Even while we were still sinners, Jesus loved us and saved us"*. (Romans 5:8) The Word of God says that the Lamb of God was slain at the foundation of the universe. Then I remembered that since my childhood, the Catholic Bishops and priests would tell my parents that god gave me special talents and I was anointed, that is why I had wanted to become a nun.

One touch from Jesus Christ my Lord and Master and Saviour made me whole.

The most precious moment of my life came in the fourth year of my sickness. This is the most blessed day of my entire life and I will live on to testify the Lord's mercy, goodness, love and grace upon me. It was summer (sunny) season and I was lying on a sofa in the living room. I was still very ill and could find it difficult to sit so I would lie down most of the times. It was one blessed Sunday afternoon around 3.oo p.m. East African standard time. After lunch I was watching then my favourite Sunday Christian Broadcasting called *"Seventh Day Adventist Programme or Hour"*. I had watched and listened to a couple of gospel singers but this was a mega-choir with very beautiful gospel music. Then as I had been watching, the music programme changed and the medium built man with a middle-Eastern look and ascent was the Preacher. I didn't know his name, and I don't remember to have seen him before, though I would see many Europeans and Blacks on Tele-evangelism. So I just fell asleep on the sofa, as he had started preaching. But all of a sudden I was woken up by something and I was very alert as if I wasn't in a deep sleep. I looked at the TV screen but I was not listening what he was talking, and my spirit was awakened and I saw the scriptures displayed as I read from the TV screen and I will never forget the exact Words of God that I read;

"And a certain woman who had an issue of blood for twelve years, and had suffered of many things from physicians, and had spent all that she had, and was no better but rather grew worse. When she heard of Jesus, she

came behind him into the crowed that pressed behind JESUS, and she touched the tarsal of his garment. For she said, if I may touch only the tarsal of his garment; I will be healed. And suddenly the fountain of her blood was dried up; and she felt in her body she was healed of that plague." And Jesus immediately knowing in himself that virtue had gone out of him, turned around in the crowd and said; "Who touched my clothes?" But his Disciples said to him, "You see the multitude thronging you and you say "Who touched me?" And Jesus looked around to see her who had done this thing. But the woman, fearing and trembling, knowing what had happened to her, came and fell down before him and told him the whole truth. And Jesus said to her; "Daughter, your faith had made you whole". "Go in peace and be healed of your affliction." (Mark 5; 25-34)

While I was reading on the TV screen the Word of God above, I sat up quickly (I believe God gave me strength). I was so captured and overtaken deeply by the Word of God, all my being was filled with life and peace again, and I felt a sense of alertness in my spirit; my soul was awakened; I felt that my entire body was quickened and I had received strength and at the same time panting and shaking. As I was still reading the Word of God in *Mark 5:25-34,* I knew this was about me! My heart was racing and I felt a sense of the presence of

Jesus Christ with me rightly embracing me with his love and new life by his amazing grace. I had received strength and energy (from God) that I made a step of faith and ran towards the TV screen, with my hands raised to heaven; I surrendered my life to Jesus Christ as my only LORD and Saviour and Redeemer and Healer. I knelt down while I was sobbing and weeping tears of joy; the joy that I have never experienced before all my life to that day; joy and peace and love that were so sweet and the feeling is so intense to explain: I felt like a newly born baby that I had never had any problems in my life. All chains and shackles of the devil were broken; I was set free and healed by the truth of Jesus; by his Spirit, he set me free from the law of sin and death. And I knew I had found the truth now and received a brand new righteous life. *(John 8:32; Romans 8:1-4 John 10:10).*

I was weeping very loudly with tears of joy, all alone by myself with my LORD JESUS CHRIST, embracing me, I loudly said, "JESUS that is me! Thank you for healing me my LORD JESUS CHRIST. That is me thank You for saving me my Saviour". I am now born-again."

While I was still worshipping God and bowing down in tears, a young maid who was between *15- 16* years of age came in the sitting room and she saw me in a state that cannot be explained; tears rolling and mixture of laughter of joy; thanking Jesus for saving me! She asked me, Aunt Christine, what has happened? I told her Jesus has saved me I am born again now! She said in a loud African tone; *"eheheheheeee" now I am born again too!"* She knelt down behind me and she raised her hands and she surrendered her life to Christ as I witnessed to her that Jesus Christ has saved me and healed me just there before I checked myself, but I believed!

I continued to bow down and prostrate for the King of kings my Lord and Saviour Jesus Christ, my healer and lover of my soul. Straight away, The Lord Jesus Christ captured my heart for his worship, I was humbled to bow down and prostrated at his feet because I knew and believed, deep down inside of my heart that he was right there with me and he is with me until the end. (*Mark 16:15-20* Jesus said to his disciples: *"Go ye into all the world, and preach the gospel to every creature. He that believeth and is baptised shall be saved, but he that does not believe shall be condemned. And these signs shall follow them that believe; In my name, they shall cast out devils; they shall speak with new tongues; They shall take up serpents; and if they drink any deadly thing, it shall not hurt them; they shall lay hands on the sick, and they shall recover."*).

Honestly, I felt so loved; I mean intense deep fullness of love that cannot be explained but that felt tangible! Right there since then I believed that I entered into a holy covenant of everlasting life and abundant life that Jesus came to give me and us all. I received (*John 10-10);* I became a brand new woman and God gave me a new name and wrote my name in the Lamb's Book of Life and erased my name from the book of death. (*Revelation 21:27 or Rev 13:8*): We find the references to the *"Lamb's book of life"* in which also are the names of all those who have been washed by the blood of the Lamb, Jesus Christ. The Lamb who has been "slain from the creation of the world" has a book in which are written all those who have been redeemed by his sacrifice- The born-again)

Still, I was weeping and sobbing tears of joy and relief: on and on thanking Jesus Christ for healing me and touching me like the woman in book of Mark *5:25-34.* While I didn't hear the preacher-man, but I was seeing and believing the Word of God as it is written in *Mark 5:25-35.* I don't remember how long it lasted, but it was the most beautiful, holy, and greatest God-encounter of my life and I will live to testify the goodness of The LORD in the land of the living. This was my first day of love for my Lord and Saviour and Master Jesus Christ. It was my first love.

I knelt down weeping and with my heart and soul and body and I surrendered my uplifted hands to heaven and wholly heartedly in my ex-fiancés small living room, while a middle-Eastern preacher man Evangelist was preaching I watched on a TV in Africa Uganda – Kampala; on a blessed Sunday afternoon and **I received Salvation and simultaneously and instantly Jesus Christ touched me, delivered me, healed me and made me whole and the fountains of my blood issue dried up instantly as I was reading and believing the Word of God.** It is all by the grace of God that I received salvation by faith; it was not by my works! This is the greatest day of my life when I received the new birth and new life. Praise God forever more! Halleluiah! My life will never be the same again! I closed the door to sickness because my God closed it by himself and by his grace, and God has opened a door of goodness and good health and prosperity for me. And this testimony was sealed in the mighty blood of Jesus Christ of Nazareth Son of God my Lord, Saviour and Redeemer; the Lamb of God who takes away the sins of the world. Hosanna in the highest. Glory be to God Abba Father.

Thank You Holy Spirit for your counsel and guidance of the Word of God in me. Amen.

This was the day of my visitation from the Lord Jesus Christ, and thanks to God that I did not miss it. This is the day that the LORD has made and I will rejoice and be glad in it. I love you Jesus who did not pass me by! Merciful Saviour, who blessed me! The Lord prepared the day of my salvation and ordained it to be extraordinary because God has good plans for me. *(Jeremiah 29:11-14)*.

In that one brief divine moment of an encounter with God, all the four questions I had mentioned before were answered and I am at peace. God is love and Jesus Christ loves me; I shall not die but live and declare the works of the Lord; Jesus Christ is the truth, The only way to God is Jesus and the way, life and truth – *so Christianity is the right faith if I could say* t worship God. I know who I am now I am a daughter of the Most High God in Christ Jesus and God takes good care of me.

The Healing Power of Jesus Christ

In *Mark 5:34* of my healing Word of God;
Jesus said to the woman, *"Daughter your faith has made you whole. Go in peace and be*

healed of your affliction." Amen, and I went, the Jesus model Preacher was still preaching and on that Word I left the preacher still preaching on TV programme; I left in faith and by faith and took a step and action of faith and the blessings I believed I got and I felt healed and went straight away to the bathroom to check and see my miracle. To God be the glory I had dried up completely as Jesus Christ had commanded me to get healed of the affliction forever. (*Mark 5:34*). AMEN.

CHAPTER SIX

AMAZING GRACE, UNENDING LOVE

There is power in the name of Jesus

Though I was a sinner, a wretch undone, JESUS loved me and he still loves me dearly and eternally. I love Jesus too because he first loved me. He touched me and made me whole, no one was with me; I was just by myself at my ex-fiancé's home, not in my parents' home; nor my siblings home; or any family member OR relative; no pastor or any born-again person was in contact with me; not in a hospital, not in a Church, not in a crusade: but just in a suburb undone dusty neighbourhood- humble place all by myself. Then Jesus hand-picked me; the amazing grace of God saved me and picked me up from the dust and pain and in-laws' rejection OR shame but sat me victoriously/triumphantly on the chairs of princes and princesses of God so that no man can boast about it and swell with pride, but to him Abba Father Almighty my God and JESUS CHRIST alone my Saviour and LORD be the glory, blessings, Honour, Wisdom and Power, forever and ever! Here I am to testify his goodness!! AMEN.

I could have kept quiet because no one was there, but I would like to honour my Holy

Father God in Christ Jesus my Lord and Saviour and pay my vows to The Lord before his people, that there is power in The name of Jesus that breaks every chains and strongholds; as I quote the Word of God by declaring:

"I love the LORD because he has heard my voice and my supplications. Because he has inclined his ear to me, therefore I will call upon him as long as I live. The pains of death surrounded me, and the pangs of Sheol laid hold of me; I found trouble and sorrow. Then I called upon the name of the LORD: 'O LORD, I implore you, deliver my soul!' Gracious is the LORD, and righteous; Yes, our God is merciful. The LORD preserves the simple; I was brought low, and he saved me. Return to your rest, O my soul, for the LORD has dealt bountifully with you. LORD, you have delivered my soul from death; my eyes from tears, and my feet from falling. I will walk before the LORD in the land of the living. I believed, therefore I spoke, I am greatly afflicted.' I said in my haste, 'all men are liars.' What shall I render to the LORD for all his benefits toward me? I will take up the cup of salvation, and call upon the name of The LORD. I will pay my vows to the LORD now in the presence of all his people." (Psalm 116:1-14)

From henceforth, I am a brand new woman
(2Corinthians 5:7); I am a child of God by the
authority given to me by Jesus Christ *(John
1:12 and Romans 8:14)*; I am completely
healed from the issue of blood (*Mark 5:30-34)*;
By His stripes I am healed from the blood
issue and all diseases and afflictions (*Isaiah
53:4-5 "Surely He has borne my griefs, and
carried my sorrows: yet I did esteem Him
stricken, smitten of God and afflicted. But he
was wounded for my transgressions, he was
bruised for my iniquities: the chastisement of
my peace was on him, and with his stripes I
was healed)*; all this is done by the Father's
touch and my life changed, *Jehovah has
touched my life and my life has become a new
one,* Jesus has touched my life my life
changed! Halleluiah!!

Towards the early stages of narrating my
testimony hope you still remember; I had
mentioned to you that I was in a life crisis
when I did not know who loves to fix all the
pain that I was going through because of the
sickness. After Jesus saving me and instantly
healing me with his healing and saving Power;
I knew and still know and believe that God
loves me. I sincerely know that Jesus Christ
calls me his daughter and I know up to now
that his presence and power is in me because
his virtue/power came out of him to heal me
and it remained in me and with me forever as I

remain and abide in him and I will bear much more fruits that endure because of his glorious Name, by the power of the Holy Spirit. (John 15:1-10)

I remember narrating to you in my journey to my redemption, that when the Lord prompted me to read the Bible, God's written Word, I asked what is the truth? I did not have any revelation to understand the gospel written in the book of Revelation; however, after my redemption and being saved and filled with the Spirit of God, from hence forth: I got to know the Truth and the Truth set me free. I got revelation to read and understand the Revelation gospel since then. Not only that but every scripture I could read or hear made sense to me and it is alive for me up to now. We see Jesus tells us about my experience in *John 6:63; "It is the Spirit who gives life; the flesh profits nothing. The words that I speak to you are Spirit, and they are life."* This is the truth that Jesus says to us, people of God believe it.

Great is his faithfulness, for the LORD is good and his mercies endure forever, says the *Psalmist in the book of Psalms 136 verse 1.*

Brethren, "I am confident that God, who started this good work in me, will accomplish

it, until the day of our LORD JESUS CHRIST."
(Philippians 1:6)

I would like to encourage someone that God answers all our prayers, questions and fills us with his love if you are in despair, help for the helpless, healing for the sick and broken hearted, joy instead of the spirit of heaviness, strength for the weak and tired and weary, and hope for the hopeless.! Give it all to him, there is nothing our good Lord can't do! *(Mathew 19; 26)* For the Lord's power to save and heal is summed up in this holy scripture: *"The Spirit of the Lord GOD is upon me; because the LORD hath anointed me to preach good tidings unto the meek; He has sent me to bind up the broken-hearted, to proclaim liberty to captives, and the opening of the prison to them that are bound; To proclaim the acceptable year of the LORD, and the day of vengeance of our God; to comfort all that mourn; To appoint unto them that mourn in Zion, to give unto them beauty for ashes, the oil of joy for the spirit of heaviness; that they might be called trees of righteousness, the planting of the LORD, that he might be glorified."* (Isaiah 61:1-3)

In his mercies and by God's grace, God gave me all that I was yearning for and they exceeded my imaginations and heart's desires. I am pretty sure and confident that more goodness is yet to come; as his Word promises us in *Ephesians 3:20-21* says; *"God can do exceedingly, abundantly above all that we may ever ask or think of (imagined); through the power of our Lord Jesus Christ that works in us, to him be glory in the Church by Christ Jesus to all generations, forever and ever. Amen." (Ephesians 3:20-21).* Testifying is explained in *Revelation 12:11* and I am doing it here it is godly: *"And they overcame him (devil) by the blood of the Lamb and by the word of their testimony".*

I received all I was yearning for at that time in a blink of an eye at the ordained and appointed time from a Holy Father's heart and touch! Glory!! Now I have written this testimony as it was written in the Word of God: *"I will stand upon my watch, and set me upon the tower, and will watch to see what he will say unto me, and what I shall answer when I am reproved. And the LORD answered me, and said, write the vision, and make it plain upon tables, that he may run that readeth it. For the vision is yet for an appointed time, but at the end, it shall speak, and not lie: though it tarry, wait for it; because it will surely come to pass, it will not tarry. Behold, his soul which is lifted up is not upright in him: But the just shall live by faith." (Habakkuk 2:1-3; 4).*

If I could have timed it didn't take up to a few seconds for me to get healed and saved, it was a dream come true, and truly God answered my prayers, there is power in the Name of Jesus. I was translated into the divine "timeless realm" by my Saviours love and mercy and grace. This is summed up in the word of God as we read it says: *"When The LORD brought back the captivity of Zion, we were like those who dream". Then our mouth was filled with laughter, and our tongues with singing. They said among the nations, 'The LORD has done great things for them'. The LORD has done great things for us (me and my family), and we are glad." (Psalm 126:1-3)* AMEN.

As a young girl who was then ill, I used to be tired, I used to labour and be in pain, but The Lord relieved me and gave me peace and rest; and he said to me; *"Come to me who are heavy laden and I will give you rest." (Mathew 11:28)* Abba Father healed me and saved me from the garbage of being tired of all the pain and affliction, shame, reproach, ooh name it all. I would like to bring to your attention that it is not only in the Jewish culture that a woman with the issue of blood is termed as unclean or laughed at; even in my culture, especially people speculated all sorts of evil perceptions and precautions; thinking that it was an abortion that went wrong, or some other superstitious things that they resent or snob you the moment you disclose your problems. So from right a tender age I had learnt to be discreet and secretive and sensitive about people though I don't display it; because it was an abomination to suffer like that.

This is a journey that has taken many years to come to pass and to put together; this is my time to write a book, for thanksgiving to Almighty God my Abba Father, to my Lord and Saviour and Redeemer Jesus Christ and I say: *"I will go into thy house with burnt offerings: I will pay thee my vows, Which my lips have uttered, and my mouth hath spoken, when I was in trouble. I will offer unto thee burnt sacrifices of fatlings, with the incense of rams; I will offer bullocks with goats. Selah. Come and hear, all ye that fear God, and I will declare what He has done for my soul. I cried unto him with my mouth, and he was extolled with my tongue. If I regard iniquity in my heart, the Lord will not hear me: But verily God hath heard me; he hath attended to the voice of my prayer. Blessed be God, which has not turned away my prayer or his mercy from me. Amen. (Psalms 66:13-20).*

I would like to pay my vows which I had vowed with my mouth without anyone forcing me to encourage someone that you will not die, also, *"I will not die but live and declare the works of the Lord." (Psalm 118:17)*

Although my sins were as red as a scarlet, but Jesus has washed me as white as snow. I wouldn't know or give reasons and can't explain the cause of that sickness, whether it was due to sins, evil and wickedness of this world; no matter what the enemy had purposed for evil My Lord Jesus Christ has turned it into good for me. He restored me and made me shine forth and see the goodness of the Lord in this land of the living. At the same time I will eat the good of the land; for the glory of God! The Word of God in the Bible says it truly thus; *"Come now, and let us reason together," Says the LORD, though your sins are like scarlet, they will be as white as snow; though they are red like crimson, they shall be as wool. If you are willing and obedient, you shall eat the good of the land". (Isaiah 1:18-19)*

Because Jesus Christ saved me and made me whole, his grace is sufficient for me and he filled me with the power of the Holy Spirit that I have more strength now in my forties than when I was in my teens and early twenties. Praise God.

There is Power in the Word of God

Brethren I would like you to understand that "God sent His Word to heal us and deliver us from our destructions."

This was stated already in the Bible of *Psalms 107 verse 20 -22* it is written: *"He sent his word, and healed them, and delivered them from their destructions. Oh, that men would praise the LORD for his goodness, and for his wonderful works to the children of men! And let them sacrifice the sacrifices of thanksgiving, and declare his works with rejoicing."*

I am doing exactly that, bringing sacrifices of **Thanksgiving;** I am praising the LORD for his goodness and for his wonderful works for me; I am sacrificing the sacrifices of thanksgiving and I am declaring the works of God with rejoicing before the people of God who are reading this book.

God Almighty did it for me in the name of his Son Jesus Christ, I am here to testify to you that whatever you are going through; believe me you, God can sort you out; just believe on God and his Word in Christ Jesus. I tell you that every Word of God is power palates; as it is written: *"For the word of God is living and*

powerful, and sharper than any two-edged sword, piercing even to the division of soul and spirit, and of joints and marrow, and is a discerner of the thoughts and intents of the heart. And there is no creature hidden from his sight, but all things are naked and open to the eyes of him who we must give account."
(Hebrews 4; 12-13)

Every word of God is power palates, I love it, because it is the Word of God that changed my life and it is what will change yours too. That is why I believe that every Word of God I speak will heal people and work in my life and their lives too, but we must continue to live by faith. We see that Peter and Paul and other Apostles preached and demons fled, the lame walked, blind people gained sight/vision, sick people were made whole; also their shadows and handkerchiefs were placed on people and they got healed (if you read the Bible in Acts); and miracles happened because of the power in the name of Jesus Christ of Nazareth Son of God and of the word of God; remember Jesus said that his Word is the Spirit of God and Life in the Book of *St John 6:63.* Right now as we read and hear the Word of God it operates on us right away. You just need to do what Jesus says you should do in his Word, you should obey and believe on him that he is the Son of God and that he is raised from the dead and he is seated at the right hand of God in heaven and he came to die and save us. And also that he is a Miracle Worker. Not forgetting that Jesus Christ will come back again.

No condemnation Jesus is enough

Jesus Christ our LORD has broken off me all shackles of chains of the devil and cancelled all the curses and cords of wickedness off my life and I am changed and I will never be condemned at all and I am set free forever. All relationships were restored and some friends came back or sought for me as I had gained good health. It was my turn to tell them that I do not indulge myself in the old lifestyles anymore I am born again. It is written that: *"There is, therefore, now no condemnation to those who are in Christ Jesus, who do not walk according to the flesh, but according to the Spirit. For the law of the spirit of life in Christ Jesus has made me free from the law of sin and death." (Romans 8:1-2)* also, read

Romans 8:34, John 3:17)

Our Lord Jesus Christ picked me from the pit and cleaned the dust off me; He washed me with his precious blood and he filled me with his Spirit and life. Though my sins were red like crimson, they became as white as snow.

How good it is to have a saviour who loves us and touches us like he did to me by a master's hand. I feel I am highly favoured and blessed. We have Christ always who is interceding for us, so I believe he is interceding for me as he is the highest greatest Priest that we have got; as it is written: *"Seeing then that we have a great High Priest who has passed through the heavens, Jesus the Son of God, let us hold fast our confession. For we do not have a High Priest who cannot sympathise with our weaknesses but was in all points tempted as we are, yet without sin. Let us, therefore, come boldly to the throne of grace that we may obtain mercy and find grace to help in time of need." (Hebrews 4:14-16)*

The Great commission and signs and wonders

There are some characteristics that describe me now; I feel good to obey the Lord and testify his goodness and obey to the great commission as it written in *Mark 16:15-18* and say to the utmost that Jesus *saves, protects, heals, provides and gives life.* He will pick you up, and turn you around, as I have testified that Jesus gave me a brand new life and turned me around, he will do it to anyone who invites him into their lives as an individual and their homes or families because he has saved most of my family too. No matter what you are going through right now as you are reading my testimony, let me assure you that trust and obey God; humble yourself at the feet of the Master Jesus and surrender your life and all your issues, he will take care of you. This is the *"General Authority of us all believers and Christians as it is written:*

Jesus said to his disciples; "go into all the world and preach the gospel to every creature. He who believes and is baptised will be saved, but he who does not believe will be condemned. And these signs will follow those who believe: In my name, they will cast out demons, they will speak with new tongues; they will take up serpents; and if they drink anything deadly, it will by no means hurt them; they will lay hands on the sick, and they will recover. So then, after the Lord had spoken to them, he was received up into heaven and sat down at the right hand of God. And they went out and preached everywhere, the Lord working with them and confirming the word through the accompanying signs (wonders). Amen" (Mark 16:15-20)

143

CHAPTER SEVEN

HAVE FAITH IN GOD

Faith in God acts, speaks, obeys

Mark 5:25-34 is the Pillar of my Salvation as an individual. I would encourage my readers to make use of the Word of God and believe it and stand on it and have faith on it in that particular circumstance and the Lord will bring it to pass.

Unlike the woman with the issue of blood, you might have an issue too; despite that, yours might be an ultimately different issue pressuring your mind. For example; *hate crime, racism, hatred, hypocrisy, double-faced, cheating, lying, envy, jealousy, greed, rumours, anger, woman beater, pride, controlling others, arrogance, insecurity, negativity; disrespect of parents or elders, (Romans 1:28-31)* or it could be an issue in form of a need for healing from sickness or pain, unemployment and financial needs, addictions and other drug-related habits, such as drug abuse and misuse, alcoholic or some sexual habits such as idolatry, pornography, promiscuity, perversion; or emotional and psychological problems such as mental health issues or depression or anxiety; Even it might be for your beloved ones in the family; and friends or neighbours. A fervent prayer of a righteous man avails much. I would like you to remember that just one touch from the Master's hand our Miracle worker the only Perfect and Holy one Jesus Christ, will make you whole and give you all your heart's desires. He will remember you and answer all your prayers, stand on his promises in his Word. This has reminded me of this song I learnt as a new believer that I would always sing: *"Standing, standing, I am standing on the promises of Christ my Saviour......* (You can find it on YouTube/online). This helps to sing spiritual hymns and learn them as well as we have learnt that faith in God acts, so you believe and do actions of faith. The Bible emphasises us to do works of faith for it is written by Apostle James: *"What does it profit, my brothers, though a man say he has faith, and have not works? Can faith save him? Even so faith, if it has not works, is dead, being alone."* *(James 2:14; 17)* Therefore, do not forget to put your faith into action, for example, Abraham who is the father of all believers.

Abraham did obey God when he spoke (*his Word*) to him and Abraham believed. He moved from his native land, and in *Genesis 12:2-3.* God promised Abraham who was very old and had no child; *"I will make you a great nation; I will bless you and make your name great; and you shall be a blessing. I will bless those who bless you, and I will curse him who curses you; and in you all the families of the earth shall be blessed."*

This is my belief that I am standing in the promises of God my Saviour. I am of the opinion that Abraham would always stand on the promises of God from 75 years of age in *Genesis 12:2-3* and he would always speak to mountains to subdue, barrenness to turn into fruitfulness and all enemies and obstacles of his life to hearken and be subjective unto the Word of God; that is why he is the Patriarch of Faith. Abraham was always a winner, and a conqueror because; he believed God who promised him that he is Yahweh, a Covenant Keeping God. Therefore, he inherited Canaan in *Genesis 13* by faith as he stood on the promises of God. Even in *Genesis 15*, God came back to make a covenant with Abram and again added more promises over his life and descendants to be. Even when his marriage was facing polygamist problems in *Genesis 16* where he had to accept his wife Sarah's request to use her slave Hagar to get a child Ishmael out of wedlock: Abraham didn't waver from his faith in God. We see in *Genesis 17* that God gave Abraham the sign of the covenant for circumcision for himself when he was *99 years* and his entire household. God commanded Abraham to walk before him blameless and he would multiply him. Again God changed his name from Abram to Abraham and he told him that he is the father of many nations; also his wife's name was changed from Sarai to Sarah. I want to suggest that this is a sign of divine restoration from God to change their names.

Eventually in *Genesis 18;* God also promised a covenant child to Abraham from his wife Sarah by which this Son of the promise was conceived in *Genesis 18:10-14* under a divine visitation from the Lord by three Angels. It is written: *"Is anything too hard for the LORD? At the time appointed I will return unto thee, according to the time of life, and Sarah shall have a son."* In *Genesis 21,* the Son of the Promise Isaac was born to Abraham by Sarah his wife who were both *100 and 90 years respectively;* this was all joy and Abraham received a reward he long awaited for 25 years! He had faith in God. The Bible says: *"And the LORD visited Sarah as he had said, and the LORD did unto Sarah as he had spoken. For Sarah conceived, and bare Abraham a son in his old age, at the set time of which God had spoken to him." Genesis 21:1-2).*

However, a decision was made for Ishmael to be sent away by Abraham and he had to obey God and have faith in him.

Furthermore, in *Genesis 22,* Abraham's faith was tested and confirmed. God said to Abraham to sacrifice to him his only son whom he loves as an offering at Mountain Moriah. I reckon that is where many believers would be confused and say; Lord, are you sure! And they would try to fast and hesitate about it. My prayer is: May God speak to me once and I may hear his voice. Nevertheless, we see that Faithfull Abraham did not question God because he believed that God is the Divine Provider (*Jehovah Jireh*). (*Genesis 22:1-14*) I want to suggest that Abraham believed God will resurrect his only son Isaac, and this points us to Christ Jesus the only begotten Son of God.

Father Abraham believed God and did whatever he asked him to do (by works or actions or obedience) for it is written: *"You believe that there is one God; you do well: the devils also believe and tremble. But will you not know, O vain man, that faith without works is dead? Was not Abraham our father justified by works, when he had offered Isaac his son on the altar? See you how faith worked with his works and by works was faith made perfect? And the scripture was fulfilled which said, Abraham believed God, and it was imputed to him for righteousness: and he was called the friend of God. You see then how that by works a man is justified, and not by faith only.*

Likewise also was not Rahab the harlot justified by works, when she had received the messengers, and had sent them another way? For as the body without the spirit is dead; so also is faith without works is dead." (James 2:19-26)

Listen to what this man Abraham unlocked! There is always a blessing and many blessings for us who trust and have faith in God, read on what God did through Abraham to all humanity; for it is written: *"Christ hath redeemed us from the curse of the law, being made curse for us: for it is written, Cursed is every one that hangeth on a tree: That the blessing of Abraham might come on the Gentiles through Jesus Christ; that we might receive the promise of the spirit through faith. Brethren, I speak after the manner of men; though it is but a man's covenant, yet if it be confirmed, no man cancels or addeth thereto. Now Abraham and his seed were the promises made. He saith not, and to seeds, as of many; but as of one, and to thy seed, which is Christ. And this I say that the covenant, that was confirmed before of God in Christ, the law, which was four hundred and thirty years after, cannot disannul, that it should make the promise of none effect. For if the inheritance be of the law, it is no more of promise: but God gave it to Abraham by promise."* (Galatians 3:13-18)

Abraham invoked heaven for God to look down on him and release a blessing that up to now, all of us are tapping or engrafted into this blessing, because; one man Abraham believed God for an extraordinary miracle of a male child Isaac.

A Saviour of the world was promised right there to Abraham that Jesus Christ is the Seed of Abraham (*Genesis 22:1-4; Galatians 3:15-18*); in whom all nations of the earth are blessed; this happened at mountain Moriah the Mountain of God where Abraham had built an altar of God to sacrifice his only beloved son Isaac; you see this only beloved son represents Jesus Christ the only beloved Son of God. God called Abraham and spoke to him and was pleased with his action of faith and obedience and it brought to us a promise of the saviour in the Beginning in the Old Testament it is written:

"Then the Angel of the LORD called to Abraham a second time out heaven and said: "By myself I have sworn, says The LORD, because you have done this thing, and have not withheld your son, your only son- blessing I will bless you, and multiplying I will multiply your descendants as the stars of the heaven; and as the sand which is on the seashore; and your descendants shall possess the gate of their enemies. In your seed all the nations of the

earth shall be blessed, because you have obeyed my voice." (Genesis 22:15-18)

Brethren I wanted us to picture ourselves in the shoes of Abraham and know that this is all our journey of faith; it is full of believing God, trials, pains, crooked and straight roads, plains, ups and downs, rivers, mountains, highways, paths and valleys, sacrifices, and offers, obedience to God, victories, triumphs, miracles and testimonies of blessings! We know that we are engrafted in the Abraham Covenant in Christ Jesus. I believe as it is written and I am hereby submitting to you to join me and believe that: *"Christ has redeemed us from the curse of the law, having become a curse for us; for it is written, 'Cursed is everyone who hangs on a tree' that the blessing of Abraham might come upon the Gentiles in Christ Jesus, that we might receive the promise of the Spirit through faith.(Galatians 3:13-14)*

Faith is consistent and doesn't give up.

Like the woman with the issue of blood in *Mark 5:25-34*; she had no option; she had spent all she owned on her medical bills and welfare! I was there too; I had been a burden to my in-laws, some friends but not a burden to my parents and siblings and ex-fiance'. God brings people around you to be patient with your nonsense!! But do not over-react and seek sympathy from people around you.

Like the woman with the issues of blood in Mark *5:25-34;* she heard that Jesus was in her neighbourhood and she did not beg for a drive or horse-ride to transport her there to meet with Jesus; she went in secret; because Jesus knows all our sufferings in secret; after all; she was not allowed to go in public places, she was considered unclean and contagious! I was there too in that place of ridicule and pain, the cars were there and a driver, but I could not afford to sit in public for I was weak and unwell; however, there was plan B to stay tuned on the Tele-evangelism and worship God and from there Jesus Christ met me at my point of need, he saved and healed me; He had mercy on me. (Please support Tele-evangelism it helps sick people in their homes I am a testimony saved by means of modern era technology).

But you know what? Jesus is waiting to remove all the labels that home office, immigration, racist comments from workmates; or on the streets, regrets from job applications or loans; your family shame and neglect, rejection of your lovers, hatred from neighbours, bullies, rumour-mongers, gossipers, slanderers, and those who despised you before when you were in the days of your suffering and trouble! Those will not be remembered no more! The Lord Jesus my God has taken away my shame or reproach and has taken away the proverbs of men off my life, for it is written: *"Son of man, what is that proverb that ye have in the land of Israel, saying, the days are prolonged, and every vision faileth? Tell them therefore; thus saith the LORD GOD; I will make this proverb to cease, and they shall no more use it as a proverb in Israel; but say unto them, The days are at hand, and the effect of every vision. For there shall be no more any vain vision, or flattering divination within the house of Israel."* (Ezekiel 12:22-24).

Believe on Jesus to help you and do not give up! Be like that woman and me, and press through the crowd who are just gone to gaze at Jesus aimlessly; but you have a purpose and an assignment which is divine from Him; He knows you by name; go on and touch on the tassel of his garment and believe in your heart and keep on whispering to yourself; "If only I can touch on the helm of his garment I will be healed, delivered, saved, blessed". So don't give up! Whichever situation you are going through; or you have done many mistakes and taken wrong decisions before in your life that have caused you that pain; repent put your life back and just reach out and touch on the helping hand of Jesus by believing, trusting and obeying God.

What else can I say? You have heard the Word of God in *Mark 5:25-34* and also you have heard and read my testimony in your era and generation now in the Lord's year of *2016* when I wrote this book; God still works miracles, If you don't know how to praise the Lord at least praise The Lord for me, because, his grace found me as I was like anybody else in pain and confusion and he saved, touched me and made me whole and well by healing me completely. Here I am surrounded by His love and holy presence every time and everywhere. We overcame the devil by the blood of Jesus by the Word of God and by the words of our testimony.

Brethren, it might be that a friend has invited you to Church; or you feel in your heart a nudge to believe; watch Tele-evangelism or God Channel or any media; just believe, even if you don't feel it, but have read this book of the testimony of the goodness of The Lord and the Good News, I ask you by the mercies of our Lord don't hesitate; believe, just press on don't give up Jesus is here for you. It might be that you are watching Tele-evangelism – don't give up or hesitate or procrastinate to give your life to Jesus. Just do it, don't wait for something bad to happen. I heard that someone said they become born again when they are so and so age, don't delay; you never know when the Lord comes back and finds you unprepared; where will you go and what will you say to Jesus?

Meditate on the goodness of the Lord

By the grace of God, I stand on the promises of God and I always find myself meditating and pondering on his faithfulness and goodness. There is the Word of God that says that: *"Remember ye not the former things, neither consider the things of old. Behold, I will do a new thing; now it shall spring forth; shall ye not know it?" (Isaiah 43:18-19a).* Indeed God did something new for me and the old sickness I don't remember any more pain or rejection of friends and relationship; I always remember his love, kindness, mercy goodness, healing, victories, favour and I am always grateful for the overflow of his Spirit like a river in me! I have forgiven people and moved on gracefully, that's why I have no time to hold people. I release them and I forgive quickly and let go and let God work in my life, 1 feel that life in Jesus is so sweet.

I was meditating on the goodness of the Lord to me while I was writing this book nearly during editing. I said to the Lord, you surely did heal me and saved me in a solace and painful place, where I was alone, I was being called names of shame, but you surely loved me, took my shame and pain away; and I can only tell people because when You saved me and healed me instantly on that Sunday afternoon, I was not in a Church or a fellowship, I was non-born-again and living with non-believers then! Lord, you are wonderful I reckoned. Then I heard the Lord speak to my heart and answer me that: "I did all this to save you and touch you and heal you in a solace place because; you belong to me alone I love you with an everlasting love! – No man will ever take the glory I did all by My own hand, and all the glory belongs to me". I replied: "Amen Lord Jesus, thank You! I know I belong to you alone and I will serve you all the days of my life, telling people this testimony and your gospel of Good News of Salvation as you are with me always until the end. You picked me from mire clay and set my feet upon a rock now I know! I love you Jesus I need you, from the moment on I will never let you go: My Saviour, My closest Friend I will serve you until the very end!" Amen.

Embrace the grace to create an atmosphere for your miracle

While you are waiting for your miracle of healing or receiving your petition; make sure that you create an atmosphere conducive for

God's visitation. You cannot control what events have happened in the past in your life but you can control your reaction. You might not be able to control what is happening even now, but you are obliged to control your reaction.

For instance, during my time of seeking the love of God and the face of God and his truth and to know who Jesus Christ was and if he could heal me; there was such a terrific speed of a created atmosphere for my miracle; which now I know that The Lord did it and it is all by his grace I thank God that I sense it and embrace it. God knows our yearning and desires of our hearts, and he gives us all our hearts' desires Bible says in *Psalms 37 verse 5*.

The Lord helped me while I yearned to know him well as I was going through the pain of sickness; to soften my heart yearned to listen to gospel music always. And I also had to read the Bible for three times; it was the first step for an entire year then; although I had not become born-again yet. I believe it had been a step by step way towards my faith. It was an atmosphere to prepare my miracle of healing; and I am confident that: God who started the good work will accomplish it in me and you too if you take a step of faith now, because; we serve a faithful God.

Therefore; be of good courage and do something to trigger your faith and inspire your spirit and heart. Your soul will appreciate it and you will feel a fundamental change in your life. For example, it became a routine for me to listen to gospel music and I even picked three songs that captured my heart and made me feel closer to God especially when I would sing them; it used to make me feel peace and rest. My Lord Jesus Christ and son of God; the Messiah saved me and healed me completely and I am securely surrounded by his holy presence – glory to Jesus Christ – if you do not know what to praise the Lord for; praise the Lord for me!!

Furthermore, for creating an atmosphere for your miracle and visitation of God, make sure to feed your mind and thoughts and heart with the Word of God. Read the Bible rather than watching your favourite soup on TV in the evening or when you are free; don't just gossip on the phone, or chat networks on

Facebook: what's up, tweeter, video games, movies, etc. Read the Bible and soak yourself in the word of God. It is not bad to be connected to social networks or media so long as you do things moderately; I am there but mostly to evangelise.

For example, I got to a point when I had to read the whole Bible that my Dad had bought me in my upper primary school; I read it twice during that time as a teenager in just one year; even though I was in pain and was not yet a born-again. I knew somehow that it is the word of God and it can do some miracles in my life. But all in all, this is the grace of God that is at work in me. It is also available for you today if you take a step of faith and search for The Lord he will be found by you. It is written: *"Seek the LORD while he may be found, call you on him while he is near: Let the wicked forsake his way, and the unrighteousness man his thoughts: and let him turn to the LORD, and He will have mercy on him; and to our god, for he will abundantly pardon."* (Isaiah 55:6-7)

Another thing is that this is the promise of God to the children of Israel as they were preparing to cross River Jordan into the promised land of Canaan. Therefore, if you want to cross from pain and lack and slavery into the miracles and success for your life; you need to tap into this promise of God which says: *"The Word of this Book should not depart from your mouth meditate upon it day and night in order to be successful and prosperous in the land that I promised your ancestors"* *(Joshua 1:8)*

I wrote for us earlier on that it is very imperative that we read and believe on the Word of God daily so that we are soaked in it. This increases our faith and blessings of God in our lives. Using myself as a living testimony, I heeded and obeyed to that inner voice in my heart that prompted me as a young person to read -on -and -on my childhood Good News Bible.

By reading the Word of God, I found some scriptures which were songs in my dialect such as this one which states that Nicodemus went to the Lord in the night to get salvation. This song used to inspire me quite a lot; in that, I would be believing and reciting the Word of God in *John chapter 3* on and on because it is the golden verse of the Bible; no wonder the Lord captured my heart to sing that song. This is where it says: *"For God so loved the world that he gave us his only begotten beloved Son, that whoever believes in him should not perish but have everlasting life."* *(John 3:16).*

Indeed thanks be to God that Jesus didn't let me perish but I received everlasting life from him. Who knows, maybe God saved me and touched me as I was reading the Bible but I didn't realise, because this Word states it clearly. My personal advice to you is please do not mind even if you do not understand anything you just read the Word of God, just obey and do it and you will live to rejoice and testify, you know why? *"Because God's ways are not our ways and his thoughts are not our thoughts, his Word does not go void but we do that, which pleases him."* *(Paraphrasing Isaiah 55:8-13)*

So many times we sin against God, but it is not that we need to run away. No one is perfect it is only Jesus who perfects everything that concerns us. We go back to God through his Son and ask for forgiveness and he is always faithful to forgive us. I will tell you that I also sin many times and I go back to cry to God to forgive me, and I know he is merciful and slow to anger and he always forgives me through his Son Jesus Christ.

However, the Word of God is so practical not only spiritual as it is written: *"Know you not that you (your bodies) are the Temple of God, and that the Spirit of God dwells in you? If any man defiles the temple of God, him shall God destroy; for the Temple of God is holy, which temple you are."* *(1Corinthians 3:16-17)*

After learning and knowing that you are a temple of God when you receive a new life from God – you cannot live the same way you used to live the old ways. You need to adapt to new godly lifestyles: pray and fast, praise, worship and honour God by taking care of yourself, no sexual immorality and other sinful ways; change for good, eat well, rest well and exercise.

CHAPTER EIGHT

OBEDIENCE IS BETTER THAN A SACRIFICE

God teaches us in his Word that, he does not delight in a sinner who gives him sacrifices; neither does he delight in a Christian who does not obey his Word. God set us a scenario in the lives of two Israel Kings, whereby Saul was rejected for his disobedience and David was anointed by God as King of Israel from the *shepherd's bush* attending to his father Jesse's flock of sheep; because David was obedient to the Word of God and God said he had found a man after his own heart. Disobedience is talked about in the Bible in the Old Testament in the Book of *Prophet, 1 Samuel 15: 22-23* it is written: *"And Samuel said, has the LORD a great delight in burnt offerings and sacrifices, as in obeying the voice of the LORD?"* Behold, to obey is better than the fat of rams. For rebellion, is as the sin of witchcraft; and stubbornness is as iniquity and idolatry. Because you have rejected the Word of the LORD, he has also rejected you from being king."

Guidance for a successful life:

Jesus reminds us in his early ministry of the first Christian Church that in this walk and journey of life we need to Love God, obey him and worship him alone. He stated that: *"Many prophets and kings have desired to see those things which you see,* and have not seen them, and to hear those things which you hear and have not heard them. And a certain lawyer stood up, and tempted him saying; Master, *what shall I do to inherit eternal life?* He said to him, what is written in the law? Now read you? *Luke 10:24-26.* Our Lord wants to remind us that we should always read the Word of God, and also put it into practice or action (obey) that is learning it by heart, write it on the door posts, teach it to our children. That is how to live successfully, it is the reason he told the lawyer to recite the Word of God from the Bible (Deuteronomy 6:4-9) by himself. So the man had to quote/recite the Torah the first 5 Books of the Bible that Prophet Moses wrote in the Old Testament. As I quote: *"And he answered and said, you shall love the Lord your God with all your heart, and with all your soul, and with all your strength, and with all your mind; and your neighbour as yourself. And he (Jesus) said to him, you have*

answered right: these do and you shall live."
(Luke 10:27-28, Mark 12:30, Matthew 22:37).

I wonder if you have ever heard of a song that says: *"to be happy in Jesus you have to trust and obey"* there is no any other way. And another kind of song says that; *"It is sweet to trust in Jesus, Oh the grace to trust in you"*

We see and read in the Holy Scriptures in *Matthew chapter 17* that Jesus took away his three favourite (inner-circle) Apostles: Peter, John and James to the prayer mountain to pray. While there, Jesus was transfigured before them. Heaven was opened and God spoke in a cloud saying: *"This is my beloved Son in whom I am well pleased: hear and obey him"*. *Matthew 17:5.*

I would like us to remember the first miracle that Jesus performed at the wedding of Cana. His mother Virgin Mary said to the people who were the wedding ushers or servants to do whatever Jesus tells them to do in order to get the miracle of good wine, better than any wine ever tasted before in the earth. Mother Mary of Jesus was the first preacher to tell us to obey Jesus Christ and believe in him if we want to please God, get miracles, live a peaceful, successfully and stress free life

without worry of what to eat or drink or feed
our families or ministries or projects such as
wedding, book launch, music album launch,
you name it: The provider is our God if we
love, trust, and obey Jesus! This is written
well in *John 2* as we read on;

"On the third day there was a wedding in Cana
of Galilee, and the mother of Jesus was there.
Now both Jesus and his disciples were invited
to the wedding. And when they ran out of
wine, the mother of Jesus said to him, 'They
have no wine. Jesus said to her, 'Woman what
does your concern have to do with me? My hour
has not yet come.' His mother said to the
servants, "Whatever he says to you, do it".
Now there were six set of water-pots of stone,
according to the manner of purification of the
Jews, containing twenty or thirty gallons a
piece. Jesus said to them, "Fill the water-pots
with water." And they filled them up to the
brim. And he said to them, "Draw some out
now, and take it to the master of the feast."
And they took it. When the master of the feast
had tasted the water that was made wine, and
did not know where it came from (but the
servants who had drawn the water knew), the
master of the feast called the bridegroom. And
he said to him, *"Every man at the beginning*
sets out the good wine, and when the guests
have well drunk, then the inferior. You have
kept the good wine until now!" This is the

beginning of the signs Jesus did in Cana of Galilee, and manifested his glory; and his disciples believed in him." (John 2:1-11

I want to tell you that the wedding ushers or servants did not question his power and authority, or try to bring in their *'I know more or pride'* to say to Jesus that 'ooh these water-pots are for purification as our customs stands'. They obeyed his orders or Word and they were humble and also respected and honoured him. When Jesus said to them to draw and take to the master of the feast; the servants did not question Jesus that eel: *"You have not even prayed or touched the water, or raised your hands in heaven and try to be loud and breaking the devour? What do you think you are doing?"* They trusted in him and obeyed his every Word and his authority and power was not questioned. That is what God wants from us to obey Jesus Christ his Son like children like these servants! God wants us to obey and trust Jesus as little children. *(Matthew 18:1-6)*

The humility was so supernatural here that even the bridegroom did not question where the wine came from, he believed that "Miracle Worker Jesus of Nazareth"; was invited to his wedding and supply was secured! So make sure that whatever you are doing, you need to invite Jesus Christ to turn your water into wine. Also, you better be content in his presence do not rush away. Many people who left early went disappointed by drinking bad wine (counterfeit miracle), yet the good wine - your miracle (love, joy, peace, the righteousness of the Holy ghost, kindness etc.); comes from heaven through Jesus Christ, so they missed on the miracle. Make sure you do not miss your miracle by doing all sorts of short cuts or anything that shows up like a counterfeit miracle. I encourage you people of God, do not be in haste, tally there and wait on the Lord patiently and he will satisfy your needs and give you all your heart's desires; I testify that he has done me well according to his Word and more is yet to come.

Speak to your problem using the Word of God

After his resurrection, Jesus said to the disciples and commissioned them and this is a general authority to us all believers; *"Go into all the world and preach the gospel to every creature" (Mark 16:15)*

Here Jesus is teaching us to speak to our problems in the day, today lives in this present day world and use the Word of God as above; every problem of any kind or any creature will go. It will go and God will do wonders and miracles for me and you. Jesus said; "He who believes and be baptised will be saved, but he who does not believe will be condemned. Therefore, believe the Word of God you will overcome your problems or any circumstances. Have your Bible at hand and within reach in order to read it as a pre-requisite.

We can read this Word of God that our LORD Jesus Christ commanded us when he was on his mission in the world with his disciples. To set a scenario for you to understand, I will give you and insight, that one day Jesus and the disciples mostly his *12 Apostles* were walking to Jerusalem and they went through Bethany and Jesus was hungry he needed a fruit from the fig. tree at Bethany, when he checked, the tree did not have any fruit because it was out of season. Jesus was angry and he cursed the fig. tree. On coming back from their destination; Apostle Peter always was curious and amazed at the word of God, so he remembered and told the Master, Lord, look the fig. tree that you cursed has dried up, it had dried up in a single day or overnight! Hear and see and believe what Jesus Christ replied to Peter and for all of us to do:

"For truly I say to you, that whoever shall say to this mountain, be you removed and be cast into the sea; and shall not doubt in his heart,

but shall believe that those things which he said shall come to pass; he shall have whatever he said." (Mark 11:23).

Therefore, my sister and brother in Christ, I encourage you to believe and use the Word of God to rebuke circumstances. God says: *"Is it not my word like a fire? Said the LORD; and like a hammer that breaks the rock in pieces?" (Jeremiah 23:29)*

The man of God Prophet Jeremiah told God, *"Ah Lord God! Behold, you have made the heaven and the earth by your great power and stretched out arm, and there is nothing too hard for you". (Jeremiah 32:17)*

Believe, have faith, trust and obey God and speak the Word of God in your circumstances as you pray and it shall be done unto you.

Salvation makes you a candidate for being filled by the Holy Spirit

In *Mark 16:17* "And these signs will follow those who believes; they will speak with new tongues. This means you get to believe Jesus and you are filled with the Holy Ghost and you start to access heavenly language called Angelic tongues".

In *verse 18* it says; *"They will take up serpents and if they drink anything deadly it will by no means hurt them (hurt us; me and you); they will lay hands on the sick and they will recover".* This elaborates clearly that the Power of Jesus Christ, the supernatural Power of God almighty is now in me and you; and upon me and you (us) who believes in Jesus and have received himself or his Power or Spirit to perform miracles and do signs and wonders. For example; Jesus is in me now; in his Word is his Spirit and as I speak to you by his Word and you are reading it now; He is here to touch you and heal you if you believe him with all your heart. We see in *Acts 2* that the Apostles and all disciples of Jesus Christ were filled by the power of the Holy Spirit. Also on a family basis, one man's family Cornelius believed in Jesus Christ. He and his family were saved and were baptised and also, they were filled with the power of the Holy Spirit, and they were transformed.

I now submit to you that while Jesus ascended in Heaven and he is seated on the Right hand of God in Heaven, but he is in us and as I preach to you and by you reading my testimony of the healing Power of Jesus

Christ; wherever you are or may be; The LORD is working right now with me as I preach to you and confirming his Holy Words through the accompanying signs and wonders and miracles as it is written in *Mark 16:19-20.*

Get passed being helped and get determined to get healed

Yes in real life some or most of us have families and friends or the institutions that support us for a time being and go with us for half way through the journey. They can give you money to go to the hospital, invite you to crusade for prayers, buy you a book as a gift like this one to read. However, you must get passed being helped and get determined to get healed by the power of the Son of God, Jesus Christ of Nazareth.

We see this in the Bible in the *book of Acts chapter 3.* As I am paraphrasing that there was a man who was crippled from birth. That means he was suffering problems that are genetic *(from birth)*; friends some problems are genetic and needs to be uprooted from our lives by the power of the name of Jesus Christ of Nazareth if you are expectant and believe for your healing miracle.

If someone is used to beg alms from others while you are crippled, they will not heal you unless you get desperate for your miracle. God gave us the authority to ask and receive, seek and find and to knock and the door will be opened for us. Please do as the word says and believing is being obedient. *(Mathew 7.7)*

I can tell you that life is full of unexpected twists and turns, but you might find this will be the best experience in life.

What were you labelled in the past? You cannot do anything about your past, but I am sure you can do something about your future by putting all your trust in Jesus Christ; because it is written; "Christ has redeemed us from the curse of the law, having become a curse for us (for it is written, *"Cursed is everyone who hangs on a tree)", that the blessing of Abraham might come upon the Gentiles in Christ Jesus, that we might receive the promise of the Spirit through the gift of faith."* (Galatians 3:13-14)

As we continue we see that the lame man was transported by his friends to the gate of the Temple which is called beautiful to beg or ask for alms. Let me tell you, my readers, there are friends and families who can transport you or support you to a certain destination or half your journey; but leave you there to sort yourself out and get healed by believing Jesus! They will take you to Church for prayers but they will not believe for you in some cases only if it is God's will. They will lift you up where you do not measure up to anything while you are in pain, in problems, and crippled. Thanks for such friends but you need Jesus, a Friend who sticks closer than a brother.

Some preachers say that this lame man was having troubles and difficulties and bad things which were happening to him that crippled his entire life; while he dwelt among the beautiful place (Temple gate called beautiful). Does this sound familiar to your situation when you go to Church every Sunday and you are still in the same problem, difficulty, circumstance or sickness? Who do you believe in? Who are your Pastors or Priests? Do you respect, love and loyal to your Pastors and Priests? Do you carry or support the vision of your Pastor or ministry? Do you fellowship with your Pastors and Priests? Do you bless them and their families or you go for only your alms or petitions? What kind of doctrine are you listening to and believing in? What is your attitude towards God? What is your attitude towards Jesus Christ; His Spirit and his Word? Do you have faith in God through Jesus Christ who is the only way, life and truth? Go deeper in faith, and you might as well help yourself rather than others helping you. Seek the face of the Lord. It starts here: *"If my people, who are called by name, shall humble themselves, and pray, and seek my face, and turn from their wicked ways; then I will hear from heaven, and I will forgive their sins, and heal their land." (2Chronicles 7:14)*

Up to until this crippled (lame) man heard the Gospel of truth of Jesus Christ Son of God preached to him; he was in the same dilemma. Whenever he saw anyone he would expect alms and had given up on himself, and he thought: that is how God created him. But on hearing the truth from Peter and John, his body was awaked and his spirit was alerted to connect to the supernatural healing of the Power of Jesus Christ of Nazareth, the Son of God and Saviour of the World. We can read it for ourselves as it is written:

This lame man would come or be brought to Church (Temple) every day for the past forty years, but he was never healed. Can I ask you to examine yourself for a moment? What is the purpose of you going to Church or praying every time you pray; is it for routine, socialising, it's kind of your work? With this kind of people, you will not find many miracles in them, because their agendas are not in the Lord Jesus but on money or jobs or routine or self-gain or lip service and they are like the crippled man at the beautiful gate. Other Christians will come to Church and get passed them and they will only have to complain instead of giving their life to Jesus and stop lip-service. *"Jesus said that a tree is known by its fruit"* when Judas Iscariot asked to join him. May the lord have mercy on us!

Like the lame man devoted to alms or begging money than praying; do you go to Church to pray or for socialising or for some other reasons? Profoundly, the lame man made a decision on hearing the truth about Jesus Christ from Peter and John, and it is a living testimony up to now. It gave headache to the Jewish leaders and Pharisees when they called it a notable miracle that is so evident that it could not be denied all over Jerusalem. Hence forth the gospel spread throughout the world even more. *(Acts 4:16)*

Amazingly, when this man believed in the name of Jesus he was healed. Can you imagine his jelly legs grow long and stronger; his ankles and feet received strength- aha who taught him to make his first step at the age past 40 years? Jesus knows us even before we are born, and brings people to help us lead us to him; Apostle Peter and John led the crippled man to take his first steps in the past-Bible. I am here to lead you now. Jesus wants to heal you today from inner wounds, and any problems you got pressing you now; and in fact he wanted long ago, change now and allow Jesus to touch you. But you need to change your company of people who you mingle with, the lame man (crippled) mingled with Apostles Peter and John. Change from your character and the kind of things and talks or conversations and films, rituals, traditions, customs and beliefs of old that you kind of hung on to can't help you anymore. I am telling you from experience, I had to change. You need to take in the new gospel of truth and the only truth of Jesus Christ and believe it whole heartedly and you will be healed and saved from your problems and destruction. They might be genetically, or whichever and whatever; they might be forces stronger than us as humans; however, they are weaker than a puff of smoke to Almighty God. And this is to show you that there is nothing that God can't do in his Son's name, the name of God's Power is the name of Jesus Christ, to save and heal lives.

CHAPTER NINE

REACH OUT TO JESUS CHRIST

While Jesus was reaching out to Jairus' house to heal his daughter; the woman with the issue of blood, reached out to Jesus for that very moment and she said: "I need this miracle now"; she touched the tassel of Jesus garment! And the power of God healed her bleeding and she was delivered from her pain, she seized the moment while they were many people or crowd who surrounded Jesus Christ but they had never touched him! Jesus Christ came for all human races, young and old, leaders, soldiers, and civilians, religious and laymen, he does not discriminate, we are all equal before God and we need Salvation. Does this sound familiar to you or people you know of? They might be in secular ways, Church goers or *pew warmers* or been in a church for so many years to *chess newcomers* or discourage them: the way some people would tell the blind Bartimaeus to keep quiet and leave Jesus alone; Jesus is ready for everyone who calls or goes to him, so do not listen to that category of people. *(Mark 10:42-46)* Just do one thing: Reach out to Jesus Christ and receive your miracle that will stand out from the crowd. Get your Salvation it is life and free for all.

Glory be unto God in Christ Jesus our Lord and my Saviour that I did receive my healing and saving miracles and both stood out from the crowd. I am humbled at the feet of Jesus Christ to reach out to him as his hand touched me and made me whole; my life will never be the same again forever! And when one is filled with the Spirit of God, there are extraordinary gifts that make them perform miracles, because Jesus said to us that: *These signs and wonders will follow them that believe" (Mark 16:17).* That is why we see that a point of contact like water prayed for heals, handkerchiefs of Apostle Paul healed, and the shadow of the Apostle Peter healed many. So I humble ask you not to believe the Word of God and the name of Jesus Christ.

Are you in the secular world? Or Church, or in religion and you had never touched our Lord because of the crowd? Then reach out to him in your heart, deep in prayer and desire his presence and call him to touch your heart; like this nameless unknown poor woman who ever touched JESUS. She had this moment of touching him before she bathed, or dressed up. Just come as you are and quietly touch on him today. Jesus says: *"Come to me, all you that labour and are heavy laden and I will give you rest. Take my yoke on you, and learn of me; for I am lowly in heart: and you shall find rest to your souls. For my yoke is easy and my burden is light".* (Matthew 11:28-30). The woman *(Mark 5:25-34)* we study here just crawled quietly without making any noise; but had made up her mind to reach out Jesus who would take away all her burdens and yokes. Would you consider doing the same in your life today? Jesus healed so many people who came to him that if they had written everyone, perhaps the Bible would be very huge; but reasonable miracles were written for you and me to know and learn a moral lesson.

We see in *Matthew 8* a person who reached out to Jesus in faith. He was the Roman Army Captain (Centurion was Commander for 100 Roman soldiers) in Israel; did not mind about his subjects or junior cadets before he goes to humble himself at the feet of Jesus. This man had faith in Jesus Christ to heal his servant whom he loved like a son- you know with someone who loves and has faith, God always intervenes quickly. When he asked Jesus to heal his servant, Jesus said: *"I will come and heal him"*. Perhaps because that's what the Israelites were used to, they take Prophets and Holy Men to their houses for them it was not new as people of God (God's Israel Nation). Even today many people are like that. And our loving Jesus is patient and longsuffering to us all people. But the Roman soldier replied to Jesus: *"Lord, I am not worthy that you (Messiah), come under my roof, (I am not worthy to receive you as a gentile who is not an Israelite despite You Jesus you are a Holy God); but speak the word only, and my servant shall be healed."* This is a combination of faith, loyalty, reverence to God, repentance and humility in order to reach out to Jesus Christ. The man continued that he was a Captain of 100 soldiers and each of them does as he would command them to do. This marvelled Jesus when he heard it and said to them who followed Him, *"Verily I say unto you, I have not found so great faith, no not in Israel"*.

This is because the Israelites used to ask Prophets to come to their houses for miracles, maybe they had a saying as some peoples' attitudes say: *"to see is to believe"* - instead of believing in God who is the Almighty and all Powerful. Therefore, Jesus condemned this attitude of *"to see is to believe"*. Afterwards, Jesus said to the Roman Captain (Centurion): *"Go thy way; and as thou hast believed, so be it done unto thee"*. And his servant was healed in the same hour. *(Paraphrasing Matthew 8:5-13)*

Be positive, forgive people and move on

People must understand that what is in the future is greater than anything I and you have ever seen in the past or gone through. Thus, good days are ahead of you and me; it is all summarised in *1corithians 2:9:* "Eyes have not seen, ears have not heard what the Lord prepares for us." Therefore, have faith, be positive, move on, God is on your side and be rest assured that you confess the word of God. For example "Greater is he who is in me than he who is in the world".

God has a plan and a purpose for your life, you are not an accident. God knew you before you were created in your mother's womb. Every one of us has an invitation for receiving God, but some people might get an attitude and do not accept him. However, when grace is upon you and you get saved, make sure you move on and know that God is with you. Forget the past, forgive and repent of any offences, a good life is waiting to enjoy it.

For instance, I know that sometimes some people who are in abusive relationships or environments or immigration or jobs get intimidated by some people or their abusers that life will be difficult for them if they would take any course of action. People used to scare me like that as a young person; but I tell you the truth: *"With God, all things are possible, whatever it is impossible for man; God is able to do it."* God has a plan and a purpose for yours life and my life and they are good plans to give you and me a future - you and I hope for, as he says in *Jeremiah chapter 29 verses 11.*

I want to let you know that nobody can force you to have a certain attitude. But life will be so much better if you will simply choose to be positive.

When you become born again; try to exhibit the peace of God within you and have self-control. Do not stir quarrels or trouble or contention, and if you were in a stressed and polluted environment with grudges and quarrels, it would be beneficial for you to move away as soon as possible or as far as you can if you would not keep quiet or control yourself. This advice also goes to intercessors. Above all things *"guard or keep your heart with all diligence; for out of it are the issues of life". (love, joy, peace, wisdom, courage, faith, and hate, malice, evil mind, theft, emotions, gossip, evil desires etc.) (Proverbs 4:23).* The devil uses those grudges and quarrels to disturb your peace. You will not have time devoted to prayer or fasting when you are fighting people *(Isaiah 58:1-5).* Except you are matured and principled to keep silent to pray and fast, then see how God answers quickly. *(Isaiah 58:6-14).* It is only the grace that sustains us; however, we should not take grace for granted.

Move on, and do things you had inspired before, and do self-development in your life; by either educating yourself into a higher institution, look for a small job or do voluntary work, even if it is in your Church.

I am blessed to be a Mentor and a Coach to many people and I have helped them back into mature higher education which they missed out due to one reason or the other in their lives as young people. I am glad that a couple of them have finished Higher Education and University. Some of them have told me that they are the first to graduate or acquire a higher education in their families. Don't give up living a happy life and continue to aspire. If I did not move on, I wouldn't have helped such people or write this book now, thanks be to God.

I know that there are some people, who had never had any setbacks, and their families added up to it; but there might be a loophole somewhere; maybe you are distressed and depressed out of nowhere? Or grieved and this left you broken? Or you have pride and it is not godly? There is nothing God can't do! Jesus will fix you even if you had destroyed yourself because of too much freedom and wealth from your parents or lovers or you earned too much money or fame that you started self-harm! Go to Jesus in prayer.

The truth is *"You can do nothing without Jesus"* as it is written in Bible in *John 15:5*. No one adds up to it in this life without a Saviour. We all need him we all need God to go through the rough patches of this world. But we have hope and faith, that Jesus Christ the Messiah said to us to be strong and of good courage. He has overcome the world and we will also live and overcome this world.

When you are going through any difficult and set back; the time comes when The Lord have mercy and restore and deliver you and saves you; therefore chose to be happy. Choose to be grateful for who you are. I did exactly that.

I did not have time to waste being negative or seek attention or sympathy from lost friendships and a relationship; I was so confident and expectant, ready to explore my new life journey I had started when Jesus saved me and healed me. I had to start rebuilding relationships again due to hurts and it was a task that needed some time, and my Lord is faithful who even healed my past hurts gradually, and I choose to be happy as the Lord provides.

I don't say that everyone must relocate to distant places; it might be that you need to take a walk in a park, or go for a weekend away, or a couple of days to a friend's house and pray for peace. Therefore, trust God to lead you on and guide you; He has the A-Z or map of the journey of our lives if you are in Christ Jesus.

Your past does not define who you are: You are destined to shine for Jesus

After the Lord Jesus Christ saved and healed me; He gave me back my life in wholeness. I prayed to God who gave me favour and strength to study, work and excel in business again. I knew that I have a destiny to fulfil and a family to look after. I knew that I have an assignment to accomplish. And I am still and forever grateful to my Abba Father God, for his Son and my Saviour Master Jesus Christ for healing and saving me. Now the sky is the limit, The Lord already blessed us in his word thus: *"But they that wait upon the LORD shall renew their strength; they shall mount up with wings as eagles; they shall run, and not*

be weary; and they shall walk, and not faint."
(Isaiah 40:31)

Be encouraged and don't give up on your tomorrows. Accept the good plan God has for you - a plan filled with hope, purpose, blessing, and increase in every area of your life! And when the blessing comes, know that your Heavenly Father sent it as he does us good!

Your experiences doesn't start when you go to Church only, but what you do in uncertain times and challenges; on your journey when you are going about your everyday life, though you cannot do them by yourself. With experience, I have learnt to trust God and call on the name of Jesus Christ to help me always! Jesus left us his Spirit (*Holy Spirit*) who is there to see me and you through and help and counsel, comfort, strengthen, teach me and you in all things. Ask the Master our Lord Jesus Christ, today to intervene on your behalf. Your beautiful transformation is only a breath away!

What you knew about me in the past like in *Luke 19:4-8* as an old Zacchaeus is not my concern today; because I have moved on and

The Lord has transformed and changed my life like the Zacchaeus of *Luke 19:11*. And this is for my good and godliness, because of the love of God in me and I am a brand new woman as the Word of God says about me in *2Corinthians 5:17*. He did this to many Patriarchs like Abraham, Isaac and Jacob, Kings like David, Queen Esther who was an immigrant; disciples and other apostles like apostle Peter, Paul, Mary Magdalena, Ethiopian Eunuch, and many others in Bible and he is still working until now.

Don't get confused, divine healing does not contract medics

In *Ezekiel 47:12,* the Scriptures talk of a river flowing from the temple and the leaves from the trees which grow along its banks are used for medicine.

Faith is not opposed to medicine and many times medicine can keep you alive even as you wait on God in faith for your total healing; especially for those ailments for which modern medicine has no answer to. The scriptures speak of a *"Balm of Gilead" (in Jeremiah 8:22)* I always have a saying that: God is the one who gives blessings for medicine to work, and even as medicine has stopped to work, then Jesus Christ will take over and accomplish the healing divinely. After all, it is God the Creator of the Universe: and Heaven and earth, so there is nothing any scientist will do that is new under the sun.

of God's personality. The truth is still moving upon the face of the earth, through you and me.

CHAPTER TEN

CHURCH OF GOD

Know who you are in Christ and that he is coming back soon

The Bible describes the Church of God as the pillar and ground of truth *(1 Timothy 3:15)*. We are the expression or representation of truth, for we are the temples of the Living God. *(1corithians 6:19)* Therefore, we are responsible for delivering people around the world into their inheritance in Christ Jesus and liberating them from every form of bondage. We are made to teach, preach and reveal the truth. For example, when you truly understand who you really are in Christ, you operate in the truth. You can't change people with their faults; It is only the truth that changes a man. This truth changed me and made me whole. It is this truth that liberated me, healed me and imparted life in me. Now I realise that I am the custodian of eternal verities, and I will never stop preaching the message of salvation to the sinner. A preacher of the gospel of truth may be the only 'Jesus' a sinner will ever come in contact with. (We are Christians or Christ-like). I and you, who preach Jesus, are the revelation of the truth of God; we carry in us the solution to every need in a man's life. Know yourself; discover who you are in Christ because you have a great responsibility to your world. Jesus is coming back soon and no one knows the hour or the day or the time. The salvation of many lives depends on you.

Whole armour of God: (Ephesians 6:10-18)

This is when a soldier of Christ enters the arena or city or political arena and fights to get the victory for the gospel of Jesus Christ. Pray about everything for you, your household, your family, your ministry, city and country. For example praying for cancelling of unemployment is a fight into an economic arena to get positive results.

Make sure that you grow in the Lord and walk by faith, have truth and do not lie again because lies are from the devil - it is ridiculing you. Read the word of God and praying always for yourself, family, ministers, leaders and others. Also, know that Jesus Christ has made you the righteousness of God in him. You should keep alert and know the tricks of your adversary the devil and stand guard. This is always explained fully in Bible as it is written:

"Finally, my brothers be strong in the Lord, and in the power of his might. Put on the whole armour of God that you may be able to stand against the wiles of the devil. *"For we wrestle not against flesh and blood; but against principalities, against the powers, against the rulers of the darkness of this world, against spiritual wickedness in high places" Why you take with you the whole armour of God, that you may be able to withstand in the evil day, and having done all, to stand. Stand therefore, have your loins girded with truth, and having it on the breastplate of righteousness; and your feet shod with the preparation of the gospel of peace; Above all, taking the shield of faith, with which you shall be able to quench all the fiery darts of the wicked. And take the helmet of salvation, and the sword of the Spirit, and watching thereunto with all perseverance and supplications for all saints." (Ephesians 6:10-18)*

CONCLUSION

Know your seasons that God ordained

When I look into my journey, there have been so many changes and steps to get further. The Lord has made me pass through hardships triumphantly by his grace and mercy. I have met many people in my life and it has been a mixture of feelings, sometimes very exciting. I am confident that Jesus is the one who is ordering my footsteps as he leads me on and goes before me; so that I can be able to carry on to live peacefully on planet earth while serving God by his grace.

God works in seasons; He moves people into your life and moves people out. Here is the key; not everybody can go where God is taking you. The higher you go, the tighter your circle will become and the more selective you have to be. God want to take you and me further, let's embrace the season and pray for the grace to handle the blessings that are ordained for this season and also to pray for the wisdom to utilise it for his divine purpose.

I say all this to glorify God in the name of our Saviour and Lord Jesus Christ and testify of his mercy and grace, love, saving, redeeming, restoring, transforming and healing power: which is all equivalent to Salvation.

I believe that I am anointed and feel that now I am *"Fully-grown-up or Mature"* Christian with some strategies, leadership skills, and the person that I am to manage the Vision that I envisage: To preach Good News of our Lord Jesus Christ for The Kingdom of God.

Today, I remembered that I have learnt a moral lesson of my values as I reflect on my past: Not to be ashamed of my Salvation, fear of God, humility - loyalty to Christ -way life and truth, I am confident that God loves me (identity), prayer, praise and worship life, reading the word (Bible), fasting, listening to gospel music, repentance and honouring my parents, never to give up focus on faith, loving and caring or giving, are my values. The Lord is gracious and merciful always to help us all.

I had to go through all these things as a training ground because The Lord was preparing me for this same reason and season; to minister to other people in my generation of the *21st Century* now and for mentoring a godly legacy for the future, in the Kingdom of God.

CLOSING PRAYER: *"Bless the LORD O my soul, and all that is within me, bless his Holy name. Bless the LORD O my soul. And forget not all his benefits: Who forgives all your iniquities; who heals all your diseases; Who redeems your life from destruction; who crowns you with loving kindness and tender mercies; Who satisfies your mouth with good things; so that your youth is renewed like the eagle's."* *(Psalms 103:1-5)*

THE AUTHOR'S STATEMENT

Christine Mbonenye Osahon is a devoted Born-again Christian whose life has been transformed by the miracle-working power of the Saviour our Lord Jesus Christ, since her time as a young person. She is now married and lives in the United Kingdom.

It has taken the grace of God to walk the journey of transformation; wholly depending on the word of God that is put into practice for her daily life, to see great exploits manifest in her life and the people that she helps around in the same line of Christian faith and new converts.

At a tender age, Christine learnt to pray and love and also help others who would need affection, helping children, youth, women, widows, refugees, and the lost souls to preach them into the Kingdom of God by spreading the good news at the voluntary level.

Christine is a Chartered Manager from Chartered Management Institute of London in the United Kingdom, and she also holds many qualifications such as Post Graduate Diploma (DMS) in Management from south Bank

University in London; Level 5 diploma in Management Studies; and a Degree in Criminology, Accounting Certificates, and ICT.

Christine Mbonenye Osahon is the sole proprietor of Jeneration of Hope. (Where Jeneration stands for Jesus -Generation) Of Hope Consultants. She is a qualified Socio-Scientist who has passions in transforming/touching and changing other people's lives through services such as Mentoring, Support, Advisory, Inspirational, Motivation and Coaching in the UK. Jeneration of Hope (JOH) Consultants is a sole trade business that conducts services which helps in changing the lives of hundreds of people to aspire; be transformed and grow; it is based in London; the United Kingdom.

This is done by one to one, groups, seminars, social meetings, crusades and community outreach. I also hope to network with other diverse minority social groups in order to bring awareness and transform lives through Churches and other minority gatherings of the Africans in the Diasporas.

Christine has also a variety of experiences working as an administrator in financial institutions, Schools, charities (NGOs) and Health and Social care establishments where her compassion and integrity characters have been utilised.

I know my testimony which is the pillar of my salvation; therefore I make it my business to joyfully tell it to people on one to one basis, and I have been going around a couple of Churches in different countries trying to testify how Jesus healed me and saved me instantly; even though I had almost given up the thought of writing a book about it.

I am so grateful to the Lord my Saviour Jesus Christ for helping me to encourage me to finish publishing this book. I believe it is all by the power of the Holy Spirit; because I remember the journey started one midnight while I was in my bedtime devotions at *12.45 am on 22/11/2012* when The Lord spoke to me to write this book and he gave me a title: JESUS TOUCHED ME AND MADE ME WHOLE". I wrote this down in my sermon notebook and I continued to pray about it. After 3 days of the Lord prompting me, I started to write my first 26 pages of this book on the night of *25/11/2012*. So it has been a long journey but I believe and hope that God who started the good work in me will bring it to accomplishment until the coming of our Lord Jesus Christ *(Philippians 1.16)*.

Now I bow down at the feet of Jesus Christ to thank God the Father and the Son and the Holy Spirit; for having healed me, saved me and let me be a witness to God's healing power by writing this book to proclaim the Good News of the Gospel of Jesus Christ for the Kingdom of God.

To God be all the glory, honour, power and blessings forever and ever. AMEN.

Christine Mbonenye Osahon.